MW01251907

HAPPINESS TOOLKIT

SHORTCUTS TO DISCOVERING HAPPINESS NOW IN AN UNCERTAIN WORLD

A Practical Guide with Actionable Steps That Will Immediately Improve Your Happiness.

By

Steven Milbrandt

© 2020

Serendipitous Finds Publications

50 Mooregate Crescent

Kitchener, Ontario, Canada

N2M5G6

HAPPINESS TOOLKIT

DEDICATION

This book is dedicated with love and affection to my parents,
Harry and Shirley Milbrandt who demonstrated the principles in
this book: authenticity, realism, loving kindness, and warmth were
provided to me on a consistent basis and an ample supply.

PREFACE

There have been many books written about happiness. I do not

pretend to have discovered a magic formula, nor do I have the

ego to suggest that I have all the answers, but I have discovered

through my own experience and the wisdom of others before me

some positive, practical and actionable advice that you can use

today.

This book is designed to be read over a short period of time --

perhaps an hour or two. The steps it presents you may have heard

before in different publications, but I will present it from my point

of view along with things that worked in my own life based on my

own experiences, struggles and triumphs.

Topics in this book range from the general to the specific. My aim

is to get you up and going fast-- the apparent watchword of

today's society. People seem to have less and less time with more

and more to do. The truth however is that within the confines of

an uncertain lifespan, we have as much time as we choose to

make for ourselves. It all depends on how we perceive the time we have, how we structure it, and how we use it to maximum efficiency. Too often, people will complain that they have no time for this thing or that thing, yet, will have no problem spending three hours playing the latest video game or a Farmville app. As well you will learn in this book, if you want to give yourself more time, the secret is to take some of it away and compress the remaining time. Paradoxically, what you are doing will expand to fit whatever time you give it.

Finding better ways to do anything is subjective. You may say to me, Steven, you are dead wrong! That is okay. It is not the first time I have been wrong, and it will not be the last. I am presenting what has worked for myself and others and will work for you too if you give it a chance.

Let us begin this journey now!

CHAPTER ONE

A POSITIVE MINDSET

How Your Attitude and Captain Picard "Make It So"

Since the invention of the printing press people have been interested in improving their lives. The category of self-improvement takes up many shelves on any bookstore or online storefront. It has been said quite rightly by self-help gurus such as Anthony Robbins, Norman Vincent Peale, Stephen Covey, Wayne Dyer, and many others that, we are what we consistently think about, and that emotion is created by motion.

If you want to feel happy in the moment, one way to do that is to move your body – clap your hands, snap your fingers or stomp your feet to the beat imagined or real and you will feel a surge of positive emotion. That, however, is momentary, and you did not pick up this book for some trait, momentary surge of positive emotion. You want, lasting change. The truth is, nothing worthwhile comes without at least some effort, and the best and lasting changes require days, weeks, and months to become habit-forming, positive results.

Before we go too far, it is important to define happiness.

Merriam-Webster, the world-renowned dictionary company, defines happiness this way:

1a: a state of well-being and contentment : JOY

b: a pleasurable or satisfying experience

wish you every *happiness* in life. I had the *happiness* of seeing you— W. S. Gilbert

2: <u>FELICITY</u>, <u>APTNESS</u> a striking *happiness* of expression

3*obsolete* **:** good fortune : <u>PROSPERITY</u> all *happiness* bechance to thee— William Shakespeare[1]

A state of well-being and contentment: joy. You can see from the above definition happiness is strongly associated with our mind and our inner thoughts. YOU are in control of your thoughts. You can create physical states in your mind and body to match what you experience on a consistent basis. That sounds simple, but it is far from simple. Many people have tried to find a formula for happiness and failed. That is because, despite this simple definition, happiness is not something to be acquired like water in a water pitcher or pickles in a jar -- happiness is. You do not find it. You nurture within yourself until it grows and matures.

"Happiness is not a station in life, a place to arrive at, it is a way of travelling. It is a matter of how you traverse the path you are on, walking each step with love."[2]

 Happiness is part of a journey in the same way that life is a journey. Happiness is the result of the choices we make. Period. Full stop. Choices. Time for another definition:

1: the act of choosing : <u>SELECTION</u> finding it hard to make a *choice*

2: power of choosing: Option you have no *choice*

3a: the best part : <u>CREAM</u> Of the cavalry the king's own was the *choice*.

b: a person or thing chosen

she was their first *choice*

4: a number and variety to choose among a plan with a wide *choice* of options

5: care in selecting

6: a grade of meat between prime and good

3

Choice involves the act of selecting something. Each of us makes choices every day. Some of what we select has no or minimal consequence on our lives, well other choices are extremely significant. Life is a series of choices – good and bad, positive, and negative, big, and small. The quote above from Wayne Dyer shows us that everything we do comes down to the choices we make. Happiness is a choice. You can choose to be happy right now where you are." But", you object vehemently, "I grew up in a bad home with harsh parents and strict rules" or, you say, "I can barely find food to live or pay my bills – "   There are always a variety of 'reasons' (justifications in our own minds), more accurately described as excuses for why something is not the way we believe that it should be. The old expression," If wishes were horses, beggars would ride" illustrates the point here that excuses, however well intended, may not be justified, and certainly will not change anyone situation for the better. Choices for example:

Whether to choose A or B?

To go to Safeway or target?

To marry Jane or Alice?

Should purchase a Toyota or Nissan?

All the preceding represents choices -- some big and some small that all of us make at some point in our lives. Every moment we are alive. We face choices. Not only do you choose what you do in life, where you go, but also what you do and how you do it. What you do and how you do it part in our decision-making is especially important.

The choice of what to be done or not done and any other decision we make comes with consequences. The outcomes of those choices determine how we feel. How we feel determines our thoughts. Our thoughts determine our actions and interactions. These become outcomes and habitual behaviors. "Everything you experience in your life is a result of your perception of whatever is out there in the world. In other words, you have to take responsibility for all aspects of your life."[4] Taking responsibility or ownership for everything that happens good and bad in your life is how you begin to take control and experience positive emotional states – also known as "Happiness".

HOW DO YOU GET TO A POSITIVE EMOTIONAL STATE?

Attitude is everything! Attitude is everything! Attitude is everything!

If you have not guessed already, attitude plays an extremely important role in the choices we make every day. Two people can experience the exact same circumstance in the exact same way and translated in their mind in an entirely different way. Why the difference? Attitude. If you believe that something is a certain way, your attitude forms either positive or negative feelings about that thing. Regardless of that thing's reality either in the physical world or the mental or emotional one, nothing exists a specific way except that our attitude makes it so. Those fans of the Star Trek franchise will remember Capt. Picard's signature phrase "Make it so" and our minds make it so by manifesting our interpretation of a reality to ourselves. Dr. Dyer reinforces this point when he says, "the choice is always your own. Anything that goes on inside your head is a choice"[5] No one has a choice about what external circumstances happen to them, but they have a choice about how they respond to those circumstances.

The choice of how we respond to any given situation is because of the attitude that we have about that thing or circumstance. Therefore, whatever you believe to be your reality will become your reality. If you form something negatively in your mind and you build it up and say this thing is going to be horrible, then it will become a self-fulfilling prophecy, not because it was going to happen that way, but because your attitude caused negative reactions to manifest themselves in your physical reality and the worst became real for you.

Many people believe in the power of attitude. Norman Vincent Peale believes so strongly in the power of attitude that his book, "The Power of Positive Thinking" became an international bestseller long before people in the medical and psychological professions exclaimed its benefits. Religious leaders such as Robert Schuller -based an entire church ministry, "The Hour of Power" on positivity and positive thinking for decades beginning in the 1980s. More recently, Joel Olsteen, Ken Taylor, Rick Warren (Pastors of Joel Olsteen Ministries, Creekside Church and Saddleback Church respectively) and other ministers of contemporary churches all know the power of positivity and creative messages to reach a fast-paced world seeking answers.

Religion and faith based systems in general, separate of any theology or whether you believe in a divine being or not, studies have shown that those people that subscribe to a faith-based system are happier people than those who do not.

Most people know that unless you have each component of an automobile design from the blueprint to the machine tooling and every component from the tires to the chassis – the motor and the electronics all designed and assembled correctly, the car will not operate as it should. In the same way, happiness begins with the right attitude. Without the right attitude happiness is not possible because belief makes it so. You are what you believe yourself to be and your attitude is a framework that everything else hangs upon. It is essential that each must practice having positive reactions to whatever happens to us rather than to be driven by our egos. Similarly, let me ask you this, how do you allow yourself to be treated by other people? Your attitude toward how other people see you and how you see other people affects the way they treat you. If someone treats you negatively and disrespectfully it is because you allow that to happen. It is important that you put a stop to that at the earliest possible moment in your interaction with others. For example, if you allow yourself to be abused verbally by others in one situation they will continue to do so if they are that type of person. Dr. Dyer again leads the way on this when he says, "If you can learn not to think anxiously regardless of your situation, you can handle anything"[6] including interactions with others and how you allow them to treat you.

Part of having a positive attitude involves the belief that things are going to go well for you and that everything in your life comes down to what kind of attitudes or beliefs you have about any given circumstance in your life regardless of its outcome. It starts with the belief that everything in your life is going to go well. Believing that – having that attitude, that positivity will bring about other positive things in your life because you have the right frame of mind to bring good into your life.

Earlier in the chapter we talked about choices and defined choice as a series of things to be chosen or selected. Those choices affect our thoughts and our thoughts become a belief and our beliefs become our actions. "Dr. Dyer says,

"Since ancestor to every action is a belief or thought then you can work on your ability to change all of it"[7]

Our ability to affect change in our personal lives is a key component to our happiness because if we were not able to change anything and we were at the mercy of whatever happened to us than happiness would be much harder to achieve. It is important to understand the power of our individual choices upon our everyday lives both in the big picture and the micro moments that we manage every day.

CHAPTER TWO

ONE AND ONLY YOU

WHAT YOU HAVE IN COMMON WITH "JABBA-THE-HUTT"

Most people born in recent years will be familiar with the hugely successful "Star Wars" (film franchise that has generated millions of dollars worldwide for Lucasfilm and most recently acquired by The Disney Corporation in 2012 and a particular character in the story called "Jabba the Hutt". Jabba is a huge, round, slug-like creature in the series and one of the most powerful crime lords in Star Wars lore. You may not first think that you have much in common with such a creature, but there is one quality and attribute that he has that you do too. Within the Star Wars world, Jabba is instantly recognizable as a large, round, lazy, sluggish creature. In the Star Wars canon, Jabba stands tall and instantly recognizable in a world of unusual creatures. In one word, he is, "unique", and, so are you!

UNIQUENESS is related to specialty, a one and only quality that makes something different and apart from the rest. This is related to exclusivity. This one-of-a-kind quality that makes something special is part of what makes happiness and its experience different between one person and another. Because everyone enjoys different pursuits, hobbies and specific interests, what makes you happy will not necessarily do the same for me. To better understand this, look again to the dictionary and define the term "unique". To be unique means:

1: being the only one : <u>SOLE</u> his *unique* concern was his own. Titled "Comfort I can't walk away with a *unique* copy. Suppose I lost it? — Kingsley Amisthe *unique* factorization of a number into prime factors

2a: being without a <u>like</u> or equal : <u>UNEQUALED</u>

b: distinctively <u>characteristic</u> :

c: able to be distinguished from all others of its class or type : <u>DISTINCT</u>

3: <u>UNUSUAL</u>

You are a unique and special person. Only one you exists in all the world. A recent online article by the BBC entitled, "What Makes Human Beings Unique" cited evolutionary development of the brain being bigger, our ability to express ourselves through creative means, our ability to think and reason, technological factors that are the basis for formation of tools and our collective creation of tools and machinery as some of the ways that human beings are different from other species on the planet. Our uniqueness is more than just being different from other species. It is about who we are as people – as unique individuals different in ways that make all of us special. Another article titled, "Ten Things That Make a Person Unique and Different" [8] is more relevant to this discussion. In the article, unique personal attributes such as: personality, attitude, experiences, habits, creativity, perspective, and tastes among other things. All these largely intangible qualities make you the person you are as distinct from others around you. In short, these attributes make you, you!

It is precisely because each of us is different in unique ways that our experiences of happiness and how we feel differ from person to person and place to place and these are slightly different culturally. This means that the way YOU experience and interact with the world around you are different from the ways that I do. Such differences add to, rather than diminish, how each of us contribute to each other and the world. Our experiences color everything including our perceptions of happiness. Happiness is not a tangible thing and although it can be measured, no one person can say definitively, "now I am happy..." Or because of this thing or that thing I am happy.

The truth is, we as humans are similar and different. Previously, it was noted that we are different in many intangible and often more indefinable ways such as personality and experience. This is only the first part of our reality though because as Maslow pointed out in his hierarchy of needs triangle diagram[9], all of us need specific and similar things.

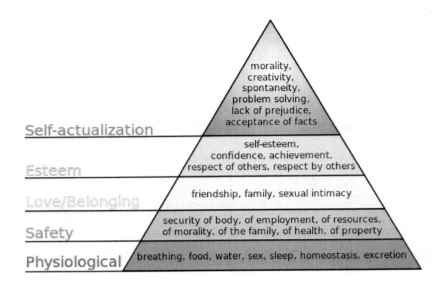

Some of these things do contribute to happiness because without them we cannot even begin to think about happiness or experiencing any kind of joy or satisfaction in our well-being. The need for food water and shelter are the most basic, followed by clothing and socialization, further up this list, where things more strongly associated with happiness are found. Dan Buetter discusses some of these elements that contribute to happiness such as pleasure, purpose and pride in his book, "The Blue Zones of Happiness" and we will explore more about this later in the book, but I bring this up here to illustrate that well we are different and the same, there are certain commonalities that unite us in terms of our quest for happiness and how we feel.

Remember here too, some of the things we intuitively think will bring us happiness, will not. The advertising industry is famous for creating a want for a product where none would naturally exist. Advertisers know that if they can create a perceived need in the parts of our brain that contributes to impulse actions before we engage our prefrontal cortex [the part of our brain responsible for rational thought], then "they" have won. The battle for what we believe will bring happiness exists in our minds and our emotions. Intellectually and rationally most people will conclude that a certain brand of beer will not, despite appearances on commercials bring us women in bikinis or high-performance sports cars. However, the battle is also between wanting more and having enough. The one thing that billionaires want but can never have is "contentment" [10] This allusion of what brings happiness, sends people scrambling for what ultimately does not matter. It is precisely because our brains are wired to seek out problems as part of our survival instinct that our desire for more, more often and better can often get us into trouble.

Humans do not need much of what we believe we do – food water and shelter are ultimately the only true necessities in life. Why then do we scramble for a better job, a bigger house, a second house, a new car, a different look or expensive jewelry? Part of it comes down to urges which are intensified by brighter and flashier products and services designed to entice and create a call to action from goods producers, advertisers and our own ultimate greed.

Everyone has individual triggers or buttons that cause them to do or not do some things over other things and this also relates to happiness. The more elaborately you live your lifestyle and focus on physical things, more and more it will take to temporally quell individual desires. Our society, indeed, individual economies, might quickly crumble if everyone began to focus on only what they needed and discarded much of the rest. What is the initial lesson here? Happiness, or more precisely, perceived happiness, means different things to different people. This is specific to societal pressures, economic upbringing, cultural differences, individual perceptions and experiences, beliefs and attitudes.

More does not usually equal better. Moderation is usually key in everything. Overindulgence often spells negative consequence on varying scales. What works for one person, does not necessarily work or produce the same results for another. We are all different – therefore, one size does not fit all with respect to happiness or any other emotion or feeling that contributes to our well-being. This reality should be a reason for celebration among various peoples around the world, but, because of our ego driven selves, this often serves to create unfair competition, struggles for power and dominance and increased levels of selfishness among some in our society.

It has already been shown that attitude is the ultimate building block to happiness and fulfilment. What we believe to be true usually becomes true for us. If we believe we will succeed or fail –

we will! Guard your mind. There is an old axiom among computer users, "Garbage in equals garbage out". The results the computer produces are only as good as the syntax of the program that derived the ultimate result. finally, for this chapter, realize and constantly remind yourself that just because you believe a certain thing is true does not mean others will agree. Differences are good. They make our world and what we perceive in it infinitely colorful. Celebrate the differences you see and welcome new opinions and beliefs.   If you are happy with a certain way of doing things, that is fine if it does not interfere or cause harm to another intentionally or not.

We are all unique and different. Similarly, we are the same in our desire to be appreciated and to love and be loved by those around us. When someone brings a belief that is different from yours, listen to it, consider it, evaluate what is positive about it and discard the rest. Be open and honest with others, while at the same time respecting their feelings and individual sensibilities. It is important to care about others and to demonstrate that concern in tangible ways every day. Be a giver, show warmth and embrace change where possible because my way is not the only way and your way may be better!

CHAPTER THREE

FIND THE INNER ATHLETE IN YOU

TRUE HAPPINESS IS A JOURNEY AND NOT A QUICK FIX

Part of becoming happy and developing that sense of well-being inside yourself involves learning that happiness is not a thing to be acquired, but rather something that develops inside you over time. Our sense of happiness is something that many believe can be acquired, like a physical object, but increasingly, behavioral scientists believe that it is something already inside of you waiting to be developed and cultivated. This may seem abstract and vague, but it is good news. if it is already inside of you, waiting to be developed, then it is available for everyone to be claimed.

One of the surprising realities of life is that our motivation happens in reverse order of the way that we believe that it does. A large majority of people on this planet believe, incorrectly, that the confidence to do something comes first and then the doing. The reality, as Neil Pasricha points out in his book, "The Happiness Equation", is that "everything you have is in reverse, you start doing and then the confidence and motivation will follow".[11] It is the doing of something that creates the motivation to do it again and the repetitive nature of doing it and doing it and doing it again creates the confidence that you and I need to accomplish any task.

It may be helpful to think like an athlete here. An athlete does not just get up in the morning and BOOM, they are an athlete. An athlete must train and train and train. Their practice and determination improve the ability of their bodies so they can react efficiently under extreme conditions and pressures. It takes many years of practice for them to become the people you see on television – the best of the best – and this elite group competes every four years to see who the best in their perspective fields is. Similarly, each of us must develop specific skills within our mental states and physical bodies that facilitate happiness. Everyone knows that if you want to make a peanut butter cookie you must follow a specific recipe. The same is true of happiness. While some people seem naturally inclined to be happier than others, no one is happy always, and, no one is consistently sad and less there is a mental or physical reason contributing to their situation. Some have developed a sense within themselves of what consistently makes them happier, and, they practice those habits consistently. If you practice happy habits, that is, doing those things that you know make you happier, then your mind and body will interpret those signals and reinforce them. Thus, good becomes better and better becomes best. It is important to consider exactly what kinds of things we can all do to improve our happiness on a consistent basis. That is one of the reasons you bought this book.

Beginning now, let us look at some specific strategies to begin to build happiness inside ourselves and all around us.

Physical Activity

Physical activity has long been associated with better mental and physical health. Exercise is part of what could be broadly thought of as "self-care". This specific category also includes things like maintaining proper rest, engaging a proper diet, being careful what you put in your body, limiting the consumption of alcohol, taking medication exactly as prescribed and developing habits that reinforce your positive behaviors and eliminate negative ones.

This type of care and attention to your own body and well-being allows you to have more time and energy to engage in the activities that you want to do. "Regular routines for basic self-care promote your ability to think clearly and give you emotional energy to tackle additional life tasks. Therefore, if you are not hungry, exhausted, hungover or overwhelmed, you are more likely to follow through rather than procrastinate."[12] It is an individual's ability to consistently follow through that contributes to a greater sense of accomplishment and a higher level of positive well-being. Many of us begin a task in earnest only to drop it a few days or weeks later because of a lack of interest or motivation. Again, if you do something repeatedly and feel mentally or physically better about it, you will be more likely to repeat the task, receive increased positive reinforcement and repetitive positive behaviors will result.

Caring for yourself not only gives you energy and motivation to do the things you value, but it also promotes positive habits for good health and increased happiness. Positive habits lead to better feelings about yourself and others because you accomplished something that you wanted to do and saw yourself following through on. "Self-care is a principal devoted to building healthy habits for energy, exercising, eating, watching your substance intake and relaxing –" [13] When positive outcomes are witnessed, habits are reinforced and repeated. To break this down further consider that "a habit is a repeated behavior that is set off by cues in your environment. [14] Habits can be positive or negative. Guard your thoughts and grow positive, affirming beliefs about yourself and those around you. Start in the positive and build on that. How can we do that specifically? Humans are/become what they repeatedly see and do. Our beliefs develop from our thoughts and our thoughts rise from what we see and experience around us consistently. The first step is to develop habits that lead to self-care. If we are eating properly (avoiding 'junk food', sugary snacks, fats) getting enough rest, exercising, drinking only moderate amounts of alcohol and engaging in meditative exercises, we can work to systematically eliminate the negative parts of our routines and schedules and replace them entirely with positive habits and routines.

In her book "Activating Happiness", Rachel Hershenberg, an assistant professor of psychiatry and behavioral sciences at Emory University in Atlanta, Georgia, outlines five principles for promoting happiness in our lives. These principles are:

1. Approach, do not avoid (a situation)
2. Set specific goals (Identify and show up for what matters)
3. Identify your top values
4. Learn to track how specific activities impact you
5. Stay on track by sharing momentary victories[15]

Ms. Hershenberg's guided approach is an excellent one. Each step in the process builds upon the previous one. Discovering how and why each of us think the way we do helps by identifying patterns of behavior. Noticing and monitoring our specific behavior means that we can potentially alter it. Instead of being reactive, each of us has a choice of how we respond in any given situation. Our awareness of our behaviors is key to the choices we make and how we respond to our behaviors in the moment. Each of us can learn about what a certain, specific behavior is trying to protect us against. A key component of this strategy, principle three, "Identifying your top values." is crucial because we can then notice whether a particular behavior is in line with our top goals and whether it moves us away from or toward those goals. Hershenberg promotes self-care throughout her book and shows how each of these principles are interconnected. For example, if one of our behavior's lines up with one of our top goals then we are more likely to follow through, be more motivated to even try and see the attempt at accomplishing it as important. It is essential to be specific in the goals that we set because this provides a measurement, something the check against, to see whether we have met and accomplished that specific thing.

Frequently, people procrastinate doing something because they are afraid of the possible outcome or they are trying to avoid perceived pain to do something. This is because, as Hershenberg points out, procrastination is an emotional decision to avoid discomfort. Sometimes, the discomfort of the moment can be accepted because the perceived outcome is greater than our present discomfort. It is also important to learn new ways to cope with tough emotions, so they do not add more stress to your life.

The key to overcoming negative emotions is being aware of them and being able to stop yourself from engaging in them at the beginning. They are traps. (TRAP that describes how we can neutralize negative emotional responses immediately.)

TRAP

1. TRIGGER
2. RESPONSE
3. ACTION

4. PATTERN

5. CONSEQUENCE (OUTCOME) [16]

Noticing what triggers our individual behaviors through monitoring them allows us to not only stop but alter them. This means that when we see ourselves engaging in a behavior we can pause, perhaps count to 10 and change the behavior to better suit our top values. Now YOU are in control of your behaviors when you notice your traps and not your ego and emotions. Although this appears deceptively simple, there are six steps to properly identify and neutralize your triggers. Here are the steps in this process:

SIX STEP PROCESS TO CHANGE BEHAVIORS

1. Notice the choice point
2. Do not Act, Breathe
3. Determine the best way to nurture yourself to feel better about the situation?
4. Choose your behavior
5. Ask how the situation served you?
6. Ask, how did the situation serve you overall? [17]

When you realize that we all have traps that we fall into, we can recognize them when we do, realize what they are and do something about them. You can learn the ways that your triggers affect you specifically. You can determine what your 'hot buttons' are. This control leads to greater flexibility and awareness.

Why does having regular routines and specific times for things matter?

Having regular routines matters because you help develop habits, hopefully positive ones, that can enhance your life and move you further toward the goals you outlined in the values you have considered earlier. For instance, the routine of exercise helps with weight management, improved cardiovascular health, a reduction of cancer risk and increases your personal longevity among other things.

CHART AND DOCUMENT

To be successful along your path toward happiness, it is also important to record and properly document:

RECORD THESE 10 THINGS ON YOUR JOURNEY TO HAPPINESS

1. Your top six values
2. Your top five habits you want to develop from repetition (repeated environmental cues)
3. Plan your daily activities in a day planner (So you can schedule things that you want to accomplish that move you toward your goals
4. Record positive and negative emotions throughout your day
5. Record your plans against the actual, eventual outcomes
6. Notice "crap" (Unforeseen negative outcomes) that gets in the way or prevents a planned activity

7. Record / chart whether most emotions that you experienced during the day were positive or negative
8. Progress toward your goals
9. Notice the specific reason why you did or did not do something
10. Write down what behaviors that you want to nurture or enhance in your efforts to move yourself towards a greater level of happiness, improved well-being and self-awareness.

You have seen in this chapter specific steps to increase your level of happiness in any activity that you are engaged. Just as an athlete must prepare and train for years before they stand on the world's podium and receive a medal, there are specific things that you can do to increase your level of happiness today!

 You have seen how emotions can affect your behaviors and how you can recognize those behaviors as they are happening, but by recognizing traps, you can change them.

We have seen that our body and mind work together and that you must establish regular routines to promote positive habits. Exercise, diet, relaxation, sleep and proper self-care all has a role to play in how you perceive yourself, others around you and essentially your well-being and happiness. Einstein said that "every action has an equal and opposite reaction" and our attitudes, how we notice and control our behaviors and emotions and our overall general physical states – that is our health physically and emotionally, all contributes to our emotional well-being and happiness levels.

ACTION STEPS

1. Review the key ideas from this chapter including the importance of determining your six top values, goal setting, recognize specific behaviors and habits and how to change them.
2. Write down your six top values – what is most important in your life?
3. Write down two to five goals that you would like to accomplish this year
4. Consider specific steps to accomplish those goals (use small, easily achievable steps) with a timeline to their completion
5. Begin to document / chart your daily activities and how they are pushing you towards your goals
6. Notice the positive and negative feelings and behaviors that you experience throughout your day
7. Use the TRAP method – TRIGGERS, RESPONSE, ACTION PATTERN AND CONSEQUENCE (OUTCOME) to notice a negative behavior pattern occurring as it is happening and use the six-step process from this chapter to change it
8. Use a journal to record your progress toward greater happiness

CHAPTER FOUR

THE POWER OF DECISION

If you have been reading this book in order, you have learned a few powerful things about happiness. First, happiness does not just happen. It takes a conscious decision to be happy. All of us make choices each day. We can choose to be sad or we can choose to be glad. The fact that we control what goes on in our own heads is a good thing. We cannot control our circumstances, but we can control how we react to those circumstances and how we feel at any given moment. Any choice, no matter how big or small is based on a decision that you and I make. Now let us look at the power of decisions.

Consider what the word decide means. To decide means:

a: to make a final choice or judgment

b: to select as a course of action —

c: to infer on the basis of evidence :

d: to fix the course or outcome of something [18]

To decide means "making a final choice or judgement". It is a 'final' choice arrived at after all the other possibilities have been considered and rejected. Many things may be happening around you, and, as said previously, people must make decisions about so many things in any given day, but, finally, you arrive at a conclusion that choice "A" is better than choice "B". A decision to put ranch dressing on your salad instead of thousand Island or olive oil is inconsequential, but a decision to study law at Osgood Hall in Toronto instead of computer science at the University of Waterloo is a much more important decision. The point is the decisions we make large and small have outcomes and these outcomes affect our happiness to various degrees.

Those decisions that are small can be made on the fly, but decisions that involve much greater consequences of outcome need to be considered carefully, all over a much larger period of time and, if more than just you are affected by the outcome, in consultation with other people you trust so that you can make an informed and reasoned decision, make adjustments, consider and reconsider where appropriate and choose wisely. If this is a decision, you are making for yourself, you must ultimately be happy with the outcome. Remember, nothing is necessarily written in stone. You are always free to make a new decision if your circumstances have changed.

Happiness is fluid. You are on a journey. This journey involves self-evaluation, internal reflection, an awareness of self, an understanding of what others expect and a willingness to reject any advice or opinion not congruent with who you are or who you are becoming along the way.

Part of becoming a happier person also means determining what happiness means for you. For one person, happiness may mean lying in a hammock in Costa Rica in the warm sunshine sipping lemonade. For another, happiness may involve making five stock trades in six months in excess over five million dollars. Whatever you believe happiness will mean for you, the true reality is probably far from what you believe. The truth is, before you can get somewhere, you must decide where you are going and the steps necessary to get you there. It has been said that "life is what happens when we make other plans". No matter how prepared you are for something, unforeseen circumstances, life challenges and roadblocks along our paths will come up like weeds in a garden. How do you minimize the risks? How do you plan for the unplannable? You step up and act regardless of your doubts and fears and past failures. Thomas Edison widely credited with the invention of the electric light bulb said when asked why he returns to the drawing board time after time said of failure, "I have not failed, I have just found ways that won't work".[19] All of us, if we are to maximize our own levels of happiness must see failure similarly. The only way to fail at something is to not try to accomplish it at all. The people who are the most successful are also the ones who have failed more often than those around them. Life is a series of successes and failures. A person is the total of everything in that person's life both good and bad – positive and negative.

It is our beliefs about ourselves and others that determine our attitude and our ability or inability to achieve or accomplish anything. If you believe you can – you will! If you believe you cannot than that too will become your reality and you will not succeed! There is power in our attitudes and a positive attitude is an unstoppable force that propels an individual to great success! Think about those people that you most like to be around. Chances are those most liked people are not negative, self-defeating gloom Sayers – they are eternally optimistic and always positive that even the bleakest of circumstances can turn around at any moment. They have made the decision to be positive. No matter what is going on around you, decide right now that nothing and no one will take away your fire! The passion that you have will drive you when others around you are telling you to pack it in, turn away and move on to safer more bankable prospects.

Anything worth doing takes work and sacrifice. The adage "When life gets tough, the tough get going", is as true today as when it was first spoken. To decide ultimately means to cut yourself off from any other possibility. To do this:

1.   Be realistic with yourself and recognize that what you are trying to do will not be easy

2. See yourself in the future with your desired outcome accomplished and imagine how this will make you feel.

3. Write down some initial ideas about how you will accomplish your goal

4. Define specific, small steps toward a measurable goal

5. Go further along your path to success in your mind and decide monthly, quarterly and semi-annual objectives

6. Write down and chart these goals and decision steps

7. Begin with simple, small and manageable things that you can complete in one to two hours

8. Define small goals (Micro) and larger (big picture) macro steps that may take weeks or months to complete

As you move towards a plan for yourself, please remember, there is no 'one right answer that goes here. Everyone is different. The steps you define for yourself and what you believe you can accomplish must not only be realistic but manageable. Small success steps over a predetermined amount of time not only makes her goals measurable but provides a timeline for their accomplishment. Make your goals as specific as possible and never say things like "make more money". The more specific you are about what you want to accomplish, the greater the likelihood that you will. If making more money is one of your goals, you need to define exactly how, in concrete terms you will do this with the skills that you currently possess or with skills that you hope to acquire.

Date	Goal	Est time to Complete	Steps to Finish	Outcome
1/20/21	Lose 5 Lbs.	120 days	define	150 lb. YOU

The simple chart above illustrates the beginning of a plan that you might develop for yourself to lose weight, specifically to lose 5 pounds of excess body fat over a period of two months. In the example above, I have set a goal to lose 5 pounds over a reasonable two-month period. Whatever charting method you use make sure you are consistent, you define realistic goals, set specific timelines for the completion and follow-through.

This book is not about goal setting, it is about happiness, but if you set goals and know where you are going it is easier to visualize the result and make it happen. Every small thing accomplished will increase your self-esteem, show yourself that you can do something and move you forward.

Happiness is not just about accomplishing the big things it is about being happy where you are. Being happy now means appreciating each moment. It means living in the present, where what is happening now at this moment – at this specific point in time.

Some people call this "mindfulness". This awareness of the present moment is not an easy skill to cultivate. People can spend years learning how to live in the present. The reason is that most of our present modern society is continually rushing, hurrying here and there. People tend to have the belief that more is better and the more things you check off the list the happier you will be. Quantity does not always equal quality. Many people believe that meditation helps to develop a present mindset because it contributes to focus and mental sharpness. A team from Massachusetts General Hospital studied the brain scans of people after they participated in a course of mindfulness and meditation. They discovered that after the course, the parts of the brain associated with compassion and self-awareness grew well parts associated with stress shrank.[20] Take time away from your regular daily activities and focus on yourself. It does not need to be a long time, but 2 to 5 minutes of mindful meditation and reflection contributes to lower levels of stress, greater concentration and the more calm and centered self. None of these steps and strategies are to be done in isolation but in combination and conjunction with other strategies.

The act of deciding something is powerful. Decide then act. This sequence sets in motion your positive attitude, your specific goals and outcomes and your ultimate success of accomplishment. Decide today that you will not continue along a negative path –

whatever one that is for you but decide today to make a change. Small changes lead to big outcomes when properly implemented alongside a well-conceived plan, set objectives and the will and determination to follow through to see tangible results that compound on each other day after day, week after week and month after month. It does not matter how many times you have tried and failed it only matters that you try and try and try again!

MAKE TODAY YOUR TIME OF DECISION AND SET YOURSELF ON A PATH OF GREATER HAPPINESS AND FULFILLMENT THAN YOU EVER THOUGHT POSSIBLE ...

Imagine your life full of infinite possibilities and promise. Believe that whatever you can imagine you can accomplish. Turn negative thoughts such as, "Oh, I could never do that" into positive affirmations such as "I can do that. You just step back and watch me!" Remove the words 'cannot' from your thoughts always and often. Choose to find the positive in EVERY situation.

ACTION STEPS

1. Decide where you are now (Your present Situation)
2. Decide where you want to be at a predetermined time in the future
3. Set specific goals as shown in this chapter
4. Make your goals small and manageable and as specific as possible
5. Write then down in a chart or timeline that you create. Personalize it and make it yours
6. Set estimated dates and target times for completion
7. Notice when you are slipping back into negative thought patterns and change those thoughts into positive ones
8. Take time daily for five to ten-minute periods of quiet meditation and reflection

CHAPTER FIVE

"The Doctor is in"

The American cartoonist, Charles M. Shultz is the creator of 'Peanuts' a syndicated comic strip series that ran from 1950 until his death in 2000. The two most widely known Peanuts characters were Charlie Brown and his dog, Snoopy. Additionally, the Peanuts gang included Woodstock, Franklin, Lucy van Pelt, Linus van Pelt, Peppermint Patty and Sally Brown. The character Lucy often set up a stand with a sign that read, 'The Doctor is In, Psychiatric Help 5 Cents". This 'Help Stand' was a unique variation on the lemonade stand and, in this book, presents a place where specific strategies for happiness can be outlined. It has already been noted that happiness is a uniquely personal thing. Elements that might produce happiness within one person may not produce the same results in another, but general principles that contribute to a positive state of well-being collectively known as happiness can be found.

Happiness as noted when it was defined at the beginning of this book is "a state of well-being and contentment, joy, a pleasurable or satisfying experience.[21] It is broadly defined as a state of well-being. Dr. Wayne Dyer describes it as a journey, and, while this is true, happiness has many layers and interconnecting ideas among different geographies and people groups. Some people wrap their happiness and even their identity in what they do – "their work". For them, what they do defines who they are as a person. They spend long hours, often at the expense of their own health trying to accomplish, to attain, or to fulfil some self-appointed work schedule that is beyond what should reasonably be expected of a person." Work-a-holics" often do not understand why another person places seemingly minimal value on what they do. They are trying to live up to the expectations of others, but, as psychiatrist Richard Feynman said, "you have no responsibility to live up to what other people think you should accomplish. I have no responsibility to be like they expect me to be. It is their mistake, not mine"[22] An underlying theme in many texts is to be who you are, that is, what makes you uniquely you. It is those things that you should showcase to others. Each of us has a unique set of characteristics, experiences, ways of thinking, personality traits, values and goals that make us special. These differences give us a certain way of approaching things that is different from others around us. Highlight those things. Show the world the person you are in all your complexities. Be a giver. Show love and genuine appreciation to everyone you meet because we are all both different and the same. Everyone has the same basic needs and wants – physical and emotional needs – the need for food shelter and clothing, the need to love and be loved, the need for a purpose and the necessity to grow and change.

Scott Galloway, in his book, "The Algebra of Happiness" talks a lot about getting the basics of happiness right because when you have those things right, other things will fall into place. He said,

"Invest early and often in the things that give you the satisfaction"[23] and he noted that it is important to "get the easy stuff right – show up early, have good manners and follow up"[24] because when people get those things right and they act in a civil manner toward others, treat others the way they expect to be treated and present a genuine / authentic self, others will naturally be attracted to them. This will contribute to our happiness because we are acting true to ourselves, contributing positively to others, and acting in accordance with our values and beliefs.

This congruency is important because if our minds perceive that we are not behaving in a way that truly represents who we are as a person then negative thoughts and feelings and emotions cannot only drag us down physically and emotionally, but they can also result in negative mental and emotional states that can manifest themselves into physical sickness and stress.

There are many applications for the smart phone today that can help you to not only gauge your happiness but represent positive things to you on a daily monthly and yearly basis. One of these Is the app "1 Second Everyday" allows you to take short video moments of your life and keep them to review later. By looking at these short clips of your life over the span of a year, you can get a small sense of what you were doing and what was important to you at that time. There are also numerous journaling and calendar apps available in the Apple App Store and the Google play store. Some of the more frequently downloaded include:

1. One Day Journal
2. Gratitude Happiness Journal
3. Mood notes
4. Journey
5. Five Minute Journal
6. Dalio

These are a few of the many applications available on Apple iOS and android phone platforms for journaling. "One Day Journal" is one of the best, with many features for rich text formats, inserting photographs and the ability to begin more than one journal within the application. Journey is another particularly good journaling and diary keeping application and it is available on multiple platforms.

Earlier in this book the importance of attitude was emphasized. Nothing helps you develop a better attitude then thinking about all the things you are grateful for on a daily and weekly basis. There is one application in this list specifically designed around recording the things you are grateful for. It is called "Gratitude Happiness Journal. All these applications are free to download and use but additional features will incur a small cost. This is only a small list to give you examples of what is available to you. These applications attempt to make journaling easier and more fun, but a simple spiral three-ring lined notebook and a blue ballpoint pen work just as well for minimal cost. What is most important is that you write.

Recording your thoughts and feelings is an excellent way to sort them out in your mind, recognize where you are mentally and physically and notice where you are improving daily. It is important to have a daily quiet time just for you even if it is only for 10 to 15 minutes. This time allows you to focus your thoughts, organize your activities and clear your mind for what you will do during the day. Writing for 20 minutes about a positive experience is believed to improve happiness because you relive the experience as you write it down and as you read it.[25] This also serves to reinforce the experience for you. In his book, "The Happiness Equation", Neil Pasricha says that there are seven ways to train your brain to be happy these are:

1. The three Walks
2. The Twenty Minute Relay
3. Random Acts of Kindness
4. A Complete Unplug
5. Getting Flow
6. Two Minute Meditations
7. Five Gratitude's [26]

Let us look at all seven of these in greater detail. The more physically active people are, the greater their happiness levels are in general. Three 30- minute walks three times a week is all it takes for you to feel better.

The twenty-minute writing exercise really makes you feel better because you are reliving what you are writing about as mentioned above. Performing random acts of kindness has been scientifically proven in happiness research studies such as the one performed by Sonja Lyubomirsky with the help of students at Stanford University when she asked them to perform five random acts of kindness for one week. Those participating in the study reported much more happiness levels than the test group because doing this made them feel better about themselves.

A complete unplug is about stepping back from work when appropriate and disengaging from those activities so that you can renew yourself and relax. For example, removing your cell phone from your bedroom or turning it off before you go to sleep, bringing nothing work-related with you on vacation and not answering any work-related emails after work.

"Getting into flow" is about those times when you are completely absorbed in the moment and what you are doing. That is, "being completely present in the present" and nothing else seems to matter that time. Being in flow occurs when you are doing something that you really want to do, and you are completely focused on it to the exclusion of everything else. Being present in the moment is also part of what meditation is all about. It is training your mind to be focused on something specific for a short period of time.

Meditation takes you out of where you are in the physical busy world and helps you focus your brain on something such as a beautiful piece of music or, in the case of guided meditation someone says words to you as you relax.

Lastly on this list is "five gratitudes". Writing down things you are grateful for shows you that you should be happy now because some people do not have those things that you list. Neil Pasricha's point is that you do not need specific things to be happy, you can, and should be happy with what you already have right now. Each of us can choose to be happy despite our circumstances. That is never easy, but it is an option always available to us and we must decide to be happy in whatever circumstance we are facing.

'Happy people do not have the best of everything, they make the best of everything!' [27]

Making the best of everything includes grim situations that usually put us on autopilot to a bad state right from the start. "Why is this happening?" or "Why is this happening to me?" are common questions people often tell themselves when things do not go as planned or go wrong according to their perceptions. The reality is that bad things happen all the time and to all types of people. The only thing that we can control in any situation is our attitude towards it and what we think about it. What may be the worst possible thing that could ever happen, in the mind of one person, may be regarded as "just part of life", to another. How you and I see a situation depends on how we can reframe it positively in our minds.

In March 2020, the world began to watch as the pandemic that would become known as "COVID-19" began to infect millions on the planet and our lives changed forever. The Coronavirus began in China around December 2019, and quickly spread to the rest of the world with alarming speed, aided, of course, by the ease at which people travel around the world -- primarily cars and jetliners. Most people see this is a tragedy because of how many people are dying because of it. Others, while they will not die, will become extremely ill before they recover.

Some people will reframe this circumstance by saying that, "yes, it is a terrible thing, but not only has it brought people closer together despite the need to be further apart, but it has brought out the best in the human spirit – cooperation, consideration, caring, working together and compassion. Although this pandemic is new to our generation, it is not the first pandemic the world has ever seen. There have been several pandemics in the last 100 years and one of the worst was the Spanish flu pandemic of 1918. At its peak, 500 million people became infected with the Spanish flu and that was more than one third of the world's population at that time and more than 50 million people died of the disease then.[28] It is also generally regarded that the mortality rate of the Spanish influenza pandemic was approximately two percent of the world's population while current estimates of the mortality rate from the COVID-19 pandemic place it at around five percent. It is more difficult to predict this as it is still currently active at the time of this writing.

Both the Spanish flu of 1918 and the Coronavirus are "novel" because no one in their era had any immunity to them. However, "One reason the Spanish flu was so lethal was there were no antibiotics to treat secondary bacterial infections, so control efforts around the globe were limited to non-pharmaceutical responses like isolation, quarantine, disinfectants and limiting public gatherings..."[29] and today medical science and infection and disease control methods have improved significantly since 1918.

It is important to discuss something as serious as a pandemic when considering happiness because people in the previous century found reasons to be happy despite what was going on around them. The people of 1919 may have had a more difficult time than those in our present because they did not understand disease and infection to the same level that we do now, nor did they have the technology that we take for granted.

> **Happy people do not have the best of everything, they make the best of everything!**

That includes EVERY circumstance – Pandemic and ALL. COVID-19 Is part of a new reality for everyone. A spirit of cooperation, unity, self-sacrifice and charity are brought out in people. These are all good things. Look for the good in everything. Even if it is harder to find, most things do have the proverbial 'silver-lining'.

It is important to look for the positive. There are multiple ways to consider anything. Why not begin with the best possible outlook? Most things in life are fluid. They say the only sure thing that can be counted upon is change. If you believe the best, the best tends to happen. If you think the worst, this tends to manifest itself also because mistakes more easily happen, negativity creates problems for anyone both mentally and physically. Neil Pasricha calls this "the paranoid survival instinct". He says that because our brains routinely scan for problems, sometimes that is all we see. Pasricha says that "we are wired for life that is short, futile and highly competitive".[30] Times have changed, no longer are we part of pre-industrial civilization like the caveman hunting for food and taking shelter in caves. In its effort to protect us, our brain sees problems where usually none exist. Our lives tend to be a constant flow of go, go, go...-- Usually however, the things that we believe to be most important, are not at all. It has often been repeated that most people, aware of their final days on this planet do not wish they spent more time at work. Most people wish they spent more time with their family and their friends. It is social connection that people hunger for most often.

The Coronavirus pandemic, just mentioned, provides the clearest example of that. Now the people are isolated in their homes, mental and physical problems manifest themselves multiple times. Technology provides a solution but not the physical connection most people crave. A hug and a handshake will most likely disappear as a form of greeting even after this pandemic and the problems associated with it disappear.

Psychology, the science of human behavior notes that we all do things for specific reasons. Peer pressure, mirroring and matching techniques [used to create rapport and likability], acceptance, group dynamics, and desire to like and be liked and basic human connections are all factors that cause each of us to do the things we do. That is why predicting human behavior generally is possible and why criminal psychologists can predict given specific factors and characteristics about how a criminal, once he/she is profiled will act most of the time. In general, we do things for money, power, and the possibility of advancement. But some people, those that Wayne Dyer refers to as "the no limit person" do things for different reasons. That person always sees the world in a way that serves them, rather than in a way that alienates or destroys them.[31] The no limit person tries to see the possibilities instead of the problems. In his book, "Happiness is the Way", Dr. Dyer says that there are three types of people in the world:

1.   those that are full of stress and worry
2.   those that do not live up to their full potential
3.   those that see themselves as having no limits

the no limit person is the person who has a different attitude toward problems. This type of person is not denying that problems are out there in the world, but they look first for solutions. Problems are not problems – they are challenges to be overcome. When you reframe the situation in your mind, it loses some of its power on you. Rather than letting failure stop you, see it as Thomas Edison did, just one example of what does not work on the road to what does. Failure should make you work harder. Welcome people who tell you that you cannot do something, then step forward and prove them wrong.

The truth is the greatest successes in history have simply failed more often than everyone else. They did not let failure and discouragement stop them. They tried and failed and tried and failed and tried and tried and tried again. Eventually, when you find what works and gather enough positive people and encouragers into your life, good things will happen! It is important that you practice having positive reactions to whatever happens in your life regardless of its outcome rather than being driven by your ego and pride.

YOU ARE VALUABLE

You are not a valuable person simply because of what you do or how much money you have. You are what you believe yourself to be. "You are always a valuable, worthwhile human being not because anybody else says so, but because you decide to believe it."[32] Your own decision to be the best possible you that you can be is not always easy, but the best things in life usually require sacrifice and are difficult.

Everyone must understand the power of their choices because what you decide to do, the choices you make in any given situation no matter how small culminate in a lifetime outcome that is either positive or negative depending upon the decisions that we have made each and every day. Make good decisions and you will tend to have positive outcomes. Although you cannot control what other people do or say, you can control what you think and feel and what you do in any given situation. Before you let your ego decide for you, do the following:

1. step aside -- do not react
2. Pause and consider your choices
3. choose to react positively even when your brain tells you to pull back
4. Do not let your desire to" be right' hurt another person for a temporary victory.
5. Look for the good in yourself and others and try whenever possible to resolve the situation peacefully and positively

When we let our ego decide anything, bad outcomes are usually the result. Sometimes we truly are our own worst enemy. Try this simple visualization technique. Imagine for a moment all the experiences that you have had over your lifetime to this point. See them in your mind. There are things that happened. Do not make the bad experiences bigger than what they were. These were a learning tool for you. Everything that happened to you, you should see is as a life lesson. Things that you consider "positive" enhance and improve your happiness levels. Those that you consider "negative" ultimately serve you because you have also learned from them. Challenges and hardships, although not desired, make you and I better people when we emerge from them. Problems are great teachers. If we did not face adversity and challenges in our lives, we would not grow or come to appreciate the positive in the same way.

There are so many people in this world. According to the latest data available from "world-o- meter" a prominent population clock, there are approximately 7.8 billion people alive on earth in 2020[33] . Think about that number 7 billion and 800 million people each with different ideas, attitudes, values, beliefs, and experiences. Most people only know what is in their immediate vicinity. Despite the prominence of world travel, people believe what they see around them and what they are taught to believe, either through experience or their personal peer groups. This leads to natural biases even if they are not always conscious biases. It is also correct to say that just because you might believe something to be true, does not necessarily mean that it is. Each of us must evaluate, based on the most accurate information available to us [sometimes it is hard to validate information] Decide for yourself what is accurate and what needs to be discarded.

"Everything that you experience in your life is a result of your perception of whatever is out there in the world. In other words, you have to take responsibility for all aspects of your life" [34]

It is when you and I take responsibility for everything that happens in our lives that we also take control because we realize that ultimately our lives are our own – that what we do or do not do, is ours to own – and the choices for happiness or its lack rest with ourselves. Believe in yourself and your ability to make good choices and your attitude about everything else will improve.

If there are areas in your life that you feel need to be improved such as a lack of confidence then take the responsibility to learn how to improve in whatever area you are struggling (either with the help of a competent professional such as a psychologist or the advice of a trusted friend that you know has your best interest in mind). Be aware that, is simply the opinion of someone else, and, as stated earlier you are under no obligation to live up to the expectations of others or to take their advice if you perceive it to be ultimately harmful to you a person or your ultimate well-being.

Lack of self-confidence for instance is the result of a lack of competence in an area. This can be improved by doing something repeatedly. The more you do something the more competent you will become and the more confidence that you will have as a result. It is important that you do not form a negative opinion of yourself that is based on the lack of your ability to accomplish something in the moment. Remember the sum value of who you are as a person is not based on any of what you do, it is who you are inside right now.

Remember that you are more than an amazing collection of cells, structures, mental pathways, muscles and joints, physical appearance or any number of other ways that you may choose to define yourself. You are not what you do, how much money you have, the friends you have or anything else quantifiably identifiable. You are unique and special. When you begin to think highly of yourself in a way that is not driven by ego, then you will see the value in others and what they can contribute to you as a person through your association with them. People change people. The friends we have are our choice. Consider them carefully because their actions and attitudes will become yours over time. Dr. Wayne Dyer also talks about the importance of being able to love yourself for who you are. He states that true self-love is not conceit because conceit is externally motivated approval seeking.[35] Everyone must guard against basing our happiness or how we act in any way on the approval of others. Think about who you want to be and how you want to be perceived by other people and practice those positive behaviors. Where you have negative controlling forces, things that some people call "personal demons", work to eliminate them from your life by confronting them because when you do, you take back more control and become a better version of you.

Earlier in this book, I said that I would present examples of what I have learned about happiness. I grew up part of a very caring and supportive family. The lessons my parents taught me echo in my head years after they have both passed away. I am not speaking as a person of privilege nor the opposite end of the spectrum, poverty. Most people are somewhere in the middle. Growing up in North America I did not always appreciate the many things that I was fortunate enough to have, but I have since learned to practice gratitude, believe in possibilities and expect the best in myself and others. I do not possess athletic ability or special talents that make me stand apart from anyone, but I do have a belief in myself and my ability to learn and grow that has taught me, especially in later years, that anything is possible. It is my responsibility to be the best here and now -- in the present. I have learned that despite anything life presents you with, that it is important to take those elements and make the most of them. If I constantly try to be my best self and strive for constant and never-ending improvement, then I win by trying and never giving up.

 My parents never gave up on me even when they discovered that I had a physical disability. Cerebral palsy. (Cerebral Palsy is defined as "is a group of permanent movement disorders that appear in early childhood. Signs and symptoms vary among people and over time.[36]) Causes vary, but CP most often occurs in 2.1 percent for everyone thousand births according to current information from Wikipedia. Personally, a lack of proper oxygen at birth and a premature birth caused it for me. I tell you this to show you that I practice the principles that I present in this book. I do not let Cerebral Palsy define who I am. Yes, there are specific things that I cannot do, but just because I cannot walk or balance myself unsupported on a chair without a back or a stool, does not mean that I do not get around very well in a wheelchair. I have also become quite adroit at climbing certain stairs, especially those with carpet and have mastered how to go down those same stairs by sliding down on my stomach. My point is that whatever situation you find yourself, you must adapt and change. See the reality of any situation for what it is-- nothing. I see possibility everywhere. No, I am not always positive, but, when I catch myself in a negative moment, I try to reframe it in a way that serves me. I try to always present my positive self publicly and encourage others along the way. Life is a lifelong learning process. Those that do not learn, ultimately atrophy and demonstrate their lesser selves as a result.

I recognize the power of a smile personally to potentially change someone's day for the better. I do not always know what happens in the lives of others, nor do they necessarily perceive my emotions or know what is going on in my life unless I choose to share with them. I researched and ultimately wrote this book, in part because I wanted to discover the secrets of happiness for myself and practice them daily. I believe, as Thomas Carlyle, the Scottish writer, once said, "Every man is my superior in that I may learn from him[37]" and everything I learn, all the experiences that I have, ultimately makes me a better person who can share that knowledge and perspective with those around me. I have a way of looking at the world that is unique to myself. It is my collective experiences, attitudes and thoughts.

The way that you look at the world is not right or wrong. It is simply different than my own. What you have learned has brought you to where you are in life and gave you a point of view. One important aspect to discovering what happiness means for you is that you remain flexible in your approaches to every aspect of your life.

Although you may have believed something to be 100% true two years ago, the same may not hold true for today because your interactions with others may have shown you that your impressions were either totally wrong or incorrect in some fundamental way. There is nothing wrong with taking the best parts of what you learned from another person and incorporating them into your life. That makes you better if you do not compromise your own values in the adoption of those characteristics.

Alternatively, you must also be able to say to someone else with specific expectations of you that you sometimes disagree. You can say something like, "I must say no to _____" (fill in the blank appropriately) because I cannot be/do what YOU think that I should. Recognize that it is okay to say no sometimes and that people with your best interests in mind will understand. If a person you are interacting with does not seem to understand, then it is just as important that you let that situation pass and move forward.

Growth in any area of your life is significant. The path to improvement is not always easy. There are often twists and turns that we do not expect, but that does not mean we should never take them. As Robert Frost so well said in the poem "The Road Not Taken:

Two roads diverged in a wood, and I—
I took the one less traveled by,
And that has made all the difference.[38]

Making a different choice for your life means that you are taking responsibility and taking control.

Making decisions and choices that are appropriate for you not only makes you feel better about yourself, but it lets others know where you are in relation to where they think you should be. Remember, where you are in your life is a result of the choices you have made, and you are ALWAYS free to change them anytime.

This chapter is about showing you specific ways that you can be happier now. It talks about everything from meditation and setting aside time for yourself to presenting strategies that will help you stay in the present and set goals that match your values. When you discover what you value, you can tailor your life to match your choices.

CHAPTER SIX

THE WORLD ACCORDING TO CORY

In September 1993, a Friday night television sitcom premiered on the ABC television network that would become extremely popular over the course of its seven-year run. It focused on young Cory Matthews and his journey to adulthood. What made viewers tune in week after week is not just that it was funny, because it was, it was also that each of these characters were relatable, identifiable and presented real-life situations and scenarios. The problems that Corey faced at school, at home and with his friends were not always solved neatly or the way that he expected, but each episode shows him learn and grow. "Boy Meets World" succeeded in large part because it did not talk down to its audience. It gave them a chance to see how Cory managed to "take on the world" week after week.

The popularity of "Boy Meets World" gave rise to a spinoff from Disney called "Girl Meets World". This Time around Cory is married to Topanga (his lifelong friend from "Boy Meets World"). This series focuses on their daughter Riley and best friend, Maya. These two girls are inseparable as best friends and must first navigate public school and later high school with their friends.

The two series "Boy Meets World" and "Girl Meets World" may seem to have in odd place in a book whose subject is happiness, but the lessons their respective characters learn, especially the life lessons taught to the characters and views of these shows equate equally to what everyone should know on their journey through life. The importance of true friendship and honesty, caring and generosity, respect for all, discovering one's place in the world and doing the right thing, even when it is not easy. These are some of the themes explored in the two "Meets World series

"Girl Meets World" presents several life lessons as Cory, Reilly's father and history teacher, talks to the class and brings unconventional history lessons before each of the students. The series emphasizes the importance of family and friends and it shows the deep bonds that develop not only between Riley and Maia but also between classmates Lucas, Farkle, Spankle and Zay.

The series target audience is preteens and teenagers but both "Boy Meets World" and "Girl Meets World" focus on the family unit in general and relationships. Adults will find both series relatable, funny and entertaining. This may not be your first choice for a Saturday evening of entertainment, but watch an episode or two, especially if you are a parent with teenagers or younger children, as episodes will present opportunities for discussion and provide an opportunity for children to open up to a parent where they might otherwise not be inclined to do.

The topics presented within each episode are things that children and teens face often in a social and school setting. They encourage exploration, challenge preconceptions encourage equality. Michael Jacobs and April Kelly created television that not only entertains but presents different points of view and allows the audience to come to their own conclusions.

The characters of Cory and Topanga that grow up on "Boy Meets World" and mature into caring, contributing adults and loving parents on "Girl Meets World" are two that some may see as unrealistic and idealistic in a world of selfish pursuits and violence that seems ever present today. The "Meets World" series' do not ignore the presence of violence, greed and poverty in the world, they acknowledge that it exists and give suggestions of how to cope, encourage and make things better. One Example is found in season three, episode eleven, "Girl Meets the Real World", Riley must debate in class whether the world is naturally 'good' or 'evil?' She comes to understand that both good and bad exist in all of us. It is up to each of us to make the right choice.

Each series acknowledges that life is hard, but with the help of family friends and trusted advisors, it is possible to make positive choices. They also show, that when things do go wrong, the people you choose to have in your circle will encourage and support you in even the most difficult times. It is especially important to "dream, believe, and 'do good' always and these words were written in big letters above the blackboard in the classroom of "Girl Meets World"

Here are a few episodes from "Girl Meets World" that are relevant to our consideration of Happiness.

Season One Episode 3 "Sneak Attack"

In this episode the topic of jealousy is explored as Lucas gives another girl attention and instead of Riley.

(Any form of negative, ego driven emotion robs each of us of happiness, causes anger and hurts everyone)

Season One Episode 13 "Flaws"

When Farkle is picked on by Billy Ross for not fitting in, Riley, Maya and Lucas rally him to show their classmates how to respect each other's differences.

This episode is important because it teaches us that it is important to respect each other's differences no matter what they are and to be kind.

Happiness comes from being true to our own values, making sure they are congruent with what we believe, recognizing and respecting the differences of others and always showing respect.

Season Two Episode 3 "The Secret of Life"

When Lucas's old friend, Zay, comes to New York, Lucas begins to wonder if New York had really changed him and he starts to keep secrets from Riley.

This episode presents the idea that "people change people" and then each of us are influenced by the people that we associate with in both positive and negative ways.

Although you cannot choose your family, who you choose to come into your life as friends will have a profound impact on you. The happiest people tend to invite positive, generous people into their lives.

This is only a small sample of lessons taught on "Girl Meets World". Everyone involved in both "Boy Meets World" and "Girl Meets World"(from series creators Michael Jacobs and April Kelly to all the cast and crew) knew that what they presented each week mattered and was watched by millions of people around the world and they were aware of the power of television to educate.

The characters in the "Boy / Girl Meets World" Series' are authentically depicted. Each has unique personalities, feelings, perspectives, attitudes and back stories. The lessons Ben Savage's character, Cory learns and subsequently passes on to his own children show that each of us can impact our own circles of influence in positive or negative ways.

Whether you agree or disagree with the author's decision to include this discussion in this book, you cannot deny the powerful force for change the television has had and will continue to have on our society. The television and the Internet have changed our society in unimaginable ways. The discussion of "fake news" brought to the forefront by US President, Donald Trump, has emphasized the need for trusted information no matter what the source. It is important to verify any piece of information with multiple credible sources and then evaluate for yourself whether it is valuable for you or not. This strategy is valuable for everything that you do and every endeavor that you undertake. Find ways to constructively and positively evaluate everything. Discard what is determined to be false and perpetuate the positive and life-affirming stories, situations and circumstances around you.

Attitude is everything! If you look for the good you will find it. Look for the bad and you will find that too, but balance is the key. Our perception of happiness is dependent upon our current state of wellness. Achieving happiness that comes from a state of wellness is, as Rachel Hershenberg notes in her book. "Activating Happiness", "is a dynamic process. While this is comprised of a set of behaviors that are shaped by your ever-changing environment" and, she suggests that "you have an opportunity to embrace your own reaction and then intervene on the level of behavior"[39] and she is right. Our behaviors help to determine how happy we are.

We are in control of our behaviors. We cannot control our circumstances, but we can control, how we react to those circumstances. There have been many accounts of people surviving in a horrific environment because regardless of what was happening around them, they found a way to change how they perceived what was happening. Some people managed to stay alive in prison camps for example, while others around them gave up and either died or became terribly sick and were killed by oppressive governments, dictatorships, fanatical leaders or abuse and neglect.

In the same way, some people see life as an adventure where every possible moment could / should be an opportunity for growth, fun, laughter, possibility, promise, challenge and new beginnings. This type of "no limit person" where the glass always seems to be half full, is the type of person that most people want to be around. They are always positive, always encouraging, always smiling and always trying to get more out of everything they do. These people are the givers that doers and the risktakers. They know that life is unpredictable. They are keenly aware that life is not always fair, but they choose to see whatever is happening around them in the best possible light.

In contrast, there are other people who always seem to be negative, look for problems, believe the worst will happen, think others are out to get them, seem to never have a good word for anyone and usually give up at the least sign of resistance. These 'nay Sayers' try to bring other people down with them to justify their negative and false beliefs. Remember, no one is positive all the time, but your goal should be that you are experiencing at least three positive emotions for every negative one that you find yourself moving towards.

Today many people, especially those in the material rich West part of the planet (North America, Europe and other western nations) are so focused on material wealth that they do not see all the beautiful things around them (nature, a beautiful sunrise, a smile from the stranger) or any number of other positive micro moments. This is because, as Scott Galloway observes society "tends to worship at the altar of innovation and youth versus character and kindness"[40] and this contributes to unhappiness because people are so focused on getting things. "Acquisition and achievements are just moments in your life in pencil", Galloway concludes, "unless you share them with the people you care about"[41] and it is the sharing of these moments that makes them special and brings us a positive sense of well-being, otherwise known as happiness.

Social media such as Facebook, Twitter, WhatsApp, Instagram, Snapchat and others, tend to make their users less happy because most people try to live up to the staged photos and mostly fake realities that they see online. People try to show their best selves on these platforms. They try to present "the perfect selfie", the best Pinterest craft or the surfboard balance on the highest wave. Some of these images are real but some are modified with programs like Photoshop. Often people will secretly wonder how their friends can accomplish so many wonderful things while they seem to be just getting by. This can lead to depression, feelings of inadequacy, jealousy and a host of other negative emotions. Much of what we see, or believe we see in our world is an illusion. The high-performance sports car that you see driving on the interstate may have been rented. The motorhome that is in front of you is probably not paid for and the pool in the backyard of some big home might still have 72 equal monthly payments attached to it. Try not to become too motivated by material wealth. You came into this world with nothing and each one of us will leave that way too.

Some people can make their profession their priority at the expense of other important things. They work long hours – 90 or 100 hours of work per week. This is not only unhealthy, but this lack of balance between work and relaxation/rest means that you do not enjoy the money that you make because your job has become the most important thing in your life. Anything can become an obsession. Work of itself, is a good and noble thing it helps to provide structure, contribute to society and gives us what Neil Pasricha calls, "The Four 'S's" What are the four S's that work provides? [42]

1. Social
2. Structure
3. Stimulation
4. Story

Humans are social beings. We like to get together in groups for common purposes and work provides a major social outlet because our workday encompasses such a large portion of it. Interacting with coworkers about work-related projects provides positive social interaction and cooperation. The workday also provides structure and stimulates us mentally physically and emotionally. It also provides us with part of our life story because one of the most common questions people ask when they first meet someone is "What do you do for living?" Our jobs help to give us a sense of purpose and the feeling of contribution. Work is important but it must be balanced with other aspects of your life such as family, spouse, exercise, faith and extracurricular/social events.

Balance in all things is particularly important. Recognize that there are 116 hours in each week. These hours can be divided into three groups of time fifty-six-hour portions -- an average of eight hours for sleep, up to eight hours for work and up to eight hours a day to do whatever you want with.[43] It is unwise to devote most of your 116 hours a week to work. If you're working for a boss, he or she will certainly not compensate you for all those hours, you will most likely suffer negative health effects and your family and friends will not have the pleasure of viewing their lives nearly as much as they deserve. An overemphasis on work will result in stress, anxiety, a compromised immune system because you are overtired and possibly an ulcer which can cause pain and other complications.

Balance between work, home, diet and exercise, moderate alcohol consumption and proper, prescribed medication intake are all important elements of your life that contribute to your well-being and happiness as a person. It is also necessary to note that too much of anything such as too much rest, leisure time or exercise can lead to their own set of serious problems.

Previously in this book attitude has been given a high priority because with the right attitude everything else will be in balance and you will be a happier person. An example of this was spoken about by Tony Schwartz and Jim Loehr in their book, "The Power of Full Engagement" where they say, "The richest happiest and most productive lives are characterized by the ability to fully engage in the challenge at hand but also to disengage periodically and seek renewal."[44] this means that the happiest people work hard but they also play hard – they enjoy themselves and they are fully in the moment with the work, at home or on vacation.

A person can have much materially and be totally unhappy while another person may be poor financially but begin every day positively and be one of the happiest people around. Why the difference? The difference is because of the war that many are fighting inside themselves. It is a war between always wanting more and being satisfied with what you have. The one thing that most billionaires do not have is contentment. Society pushes everyone toward more and better and the feeling that unless you have the latest thing that you are somehow lacking. This is totally untrue and is the cause of much unhappiness. Everyone is generally greedy by nature, but we must fight /resist that nature. We must see that what we have is usually enough. Some people can pull this off, but others struggle constantly with this idea.

Being happy now is a choice! I repeat this now because it is so important. Our choices can bring us happiness or extreme displeasure and depression. If you find that something you are doing is not bringing you happiness, then do your best to either stop doing that thing or replace it with something that does make you happier even if it means lower income or in the case of some hobbies, no income at all. If you do something for the pure joy of it, there is much more value in that. Do not do something because other people want you to, do it because you want to, and it makes you happy. Some people take a lifetime to learn that lesson. Many well-intentioned people may criticize your choices, but you are not obligated to live the life they want. Make yourself happy first and anything else is a side benefit.

ACTION STEPS

1. What popular television sitcom of the early 90s tied valuable lessons to adolescents and teens about life and happiness?

2. What was the name of its spinoff series created by Disney then introduced a whole new generation to Cory Matthews?

3. Why is it important to consider all sources of information, validating it with known sources of accurate information and deciding for yourself what is true?

4. What are the two most common types of people in our society according to this chapter?

5. What is one major reason why people are not happy today according to Scott Galloway?

6. Why is balance an important element of happiness?

7. Remember that work provides for things. It provides a social outlet, structure, stimulation and the opportunity for story.

8. Recognize that happiness is a choice!

CHAPTER SEVEN

MORK WILL LEAD THE WAY

Remember the 70s television series that ran from 1978 to 1982 that starred Robin Williams and Pam Dawber, "Mork and Mindy". The show's "off-the-wall" concept of a likeable but misguided alien who crash lands on earth and finds a wonderful friend in the character of Mindy. Mork, who drinks orange juice with his finger, obviously finds adapting to earth customs difficult, but most often the optimist, he often succeeds despite himself.

Mindy McConnell and "Mork from Ork" lived, according to show writers, in Boulder Colorado. Boulder is known for its association with gold seekers, the location of the main campus of the University of Colorado – the state's largest university, is located in Boulder, and increasingly Boulder is becoming known as one of the best places to live in the United States. Mork must have intuitively known that he landed his spacecraft in a good place when he crash lands his Orkan spacecraft in Boulder.

Our" happiness toolkit" has shown your ways that you can develop happy habits – that happiness is a choice and that happiness is not found in money and material things. Increasingly though, happiness at least in some quantifiable way can be found in "places". Boulder Colorado has been the site of designed "happy community" for many years. This city that boasts a population of some 107, 353[45] according to a recent estimate.

This city, although it is small with an area of just 25.5 mi.^{2} has clearly become known as one of the happiest places in the US because of laws enacted by city planners who knew the value of green space and environmentally friendly policies. Its leaders have enacted laws to protect its forests and, as early as 1967, Waldron introduced the "Boulder greenbelt sales tax". This tax was billed as an "initiative to promote and facilitate the development of green spaces in the state".[46] Boulder also has over 45 000 acres of forest around it and 300 miles of bike paths.

Since "good health" (a relatively generic label for one's bodily condition) has long been equated with exercise, Boulder, Colorado is a winner here too because "there are more people per capita who walk to work in Boulder than any other city in the United States".[47]

Why am I spending all this time talking about Boulder Colorado?

I am talking to you about Boulder Colorado because there are specific places in the world where people tend to be happier and this is largely due to the efforts of these places to make them this way.

In one of the first books of its kind, "The Blue Zones of Happiness", author Dan Buetter, (the founder of "Blue Zones" -- an organization whose goal is 'to help Americans live longer, healthier and happier lives' [48] explains through over thirty-five years of collected scientific research that there are specific places on earth where people are living longer, healthier and much more happiness filled lives than other places on this planet. While specific statistical data is beyond the scope of this book, you can learn more about it and see all the numbers for yourself at www.bluezones.com

Much of the information that is the basis for this chapter, as a means of full disclosure, is derived from information found in this book, although, modification and artistic license from this author, well not altering dates or numbers, is possible.

Full credit for all sources used in this book including Mr. Buettner's can be found in the biographical reference and end notes sections which is located at the back of this book.

Location and the physical place where you live will not, in itself, bring happiness, but it can act as a contributing factor to that happiness because something as simple as living in a warm temperate climate will make life more enjoyable and, at its most basic level, easier.

There are certain places such as California in the western portion of the United States that boasts a relatively mild temperate climate in its southern portion but, in its northern areas, snow and colder weather can often be found. It is precisely because of its mild climate generally that California as a state has one of the highest populations in the United States at approximately 39.5 million residents across 163, 696 square miles[49] California though is not high among the happiest places to live in the world. That distinction belongs to Denmark, Singapore, and Mexico[50] These three places consistently rank high on indexes like the Gallop Sharecare Well-Being Index that measures 55 facets of health and well-being across five distinct elements including purpose, social, financial community and physical.

Alongside the blue zones project, there is also the "Consensus Project" a sub-project of" Bluezones" that contributes overall data to this endeavor.

It is reasonable to conclude that before anyone can determine or rank "the world's happiest places", someone needs to determine what it is that makes people the happiest scientifically.

You can take a personalized version of the Blue Zones of Happiness test online for yourself at:

https://apps.bluezones.com/en/happiness

This task is part of the criteria used to determine how happy a place is based on specific qualities or attributes. It is based on Mr. Buetter's research in determining happiness levels based on three specific elements. These are pleasure, purpose and pride.[51]

Pleasure based happiness is defined as experiential or "positive effect happiness

Purpose based happiness is endemic.

Let us again define the terms here

Endemic is defined as:

Definition of *endemic*

1a: belonging or native to a particular people or country

b: characteristic of or prevalent in a particular field, area, or environment problems *endemic* to translation the self-indulgence *endemic* in the film industry

2: restricted or peculiar to a locality or region *endemic* diseases an *endemic* species

Therefore, purpose-based happiness is specific to what is "characteristic to a particular field or area. It is something that you define personally. The Okinawa people who live in Okinawa, Japan (who are among the oldest living women in the world) know their purpose in life. They define it for themselves at an incredibly early age. Whatever that purpose is for them specifically, they call their purpose "their 'IKIGAI'

So that you become a happier person, you must discover your <u>IKIGAI</u>

Do you know your life's purpose? How would you define it for yourself?

The third happiness strand as defined by Dan Buettner is pride based. Pride based happiness is defined quantitatively with a tool called "the "Cantril self-anchoring and thriving scale" and is based in a ranking of zero through ten.[52] Scientists call this method of measuring happiness 'evaluative' because each person is out to determine rankings based on specific measurements.

All this data, considered based upon pleasure, purpose, and pride can, accurately determine on a qualitative and quantitative basis how happy someone is scientifically.

Buetter also seems to agree with Wayne Dyer in asserting that "much more than genetics affects happiness", like Dyer he suggests that "how we think and what we do" matter significantly.

If you took the time to take the "Blue Zones of Happiness" test by going to the website noted above and here

https://apps.bluezones.com/en/happiness

You will get a specific ranking of your happiness level based on how you answer the questions in the survey. It is important that you are as completely honest with yourself as possible when you answer these questions so that you get the most accurate reading of your happiness level that you can.

His book, "The Blue Zones of Happiness" can be distilled down into what Dan calls "The Power 9 of Happiness"

THE POWER 9 of Happiness are: [53]

1. Love someone
2. Maintain an inner circle
3. Engage in life
4. Learn how to be likeable
5. Move naturally
6. Look forward in life
7. Sleep 7+ hours a day

8. Shape / create your surroundings (environment)

9. Belong – Find the right community that supports you

these nine principles may seem overly simplistic with things like loving someone and engaging in life will certainly make a happier person. When you engage in activities like these you are taking your eyes off yourself and putting them on other people, community groups and your friends, defined in the list as "your inner circle" and doing things that promote healthy lifestyle such as exercise, diet and proper rest all combine to form a better, happier you!

If we look closer at a couple of specific elements let us, consider how you might find your purpose for example.

Richard Leider teaches a simple formula that will help you discover your purpose. He says, G + P + V = C

Now for the key to understanding the formula

G = Gifts (what abilities you have)

P= Passion (What excites you)

V = Values (What is most important to you!)

C = Calling or Purpose

To put it all together – Gifts + Passion + Values = Your Purpose one of the questions most frequently asked by humans for millennia is "Why am I here?" People are really asking, "What's my purpose?" It is a simple, but complex question. The answers are different depending upon whom you ask. Whatever you believe your purpose is, that is especially important because it gives you a sense of who you are and what you are about.

Knowing your purpose means that you can look for opportunities to use your gifts and talents toward a meaningful goal that is in line with your values.

The best place to start is usually at the beginning. Here is a simple checklist to make sure that you are on track and moving forward toward the person you ultimately want to become.

- Write down your five top values
- Determine where your life is now relative to where you want to be in two years, five years and 10 years' time.
- Decide what you can do today to move in the direction of your short- and longer-term goals
- Take at least one small step each day toward at least one of your goals
- Monitor your progress – you can put this in a simple chart or write in a journal so that you can see positive changes

- Most people cannot do everything necessary in isolation (solo) so connect with someone you trust so that you have accountability.
- Progress may be slow initially; this often builds as you work your way through your list
- set up simple rewards for yourself so that you are more inclined to follow through when things become more difficult.
- Everyone needs encouragement along the journey of life. For every negative criticism you give another, try to counterbalance this with at least three positive affirmations or statements.

The "Blue Zones of Happiness" quiz that was referenced earlier in this chapter is a good starting point to determine roughly how happy you are presently. Many people are not where they would like to be on the happiness scale and that is okay. Progress can be small at first. Positive benefits can spur you on to greater effort.

Top Values	Top Goals	Date Begun	Date Completed	Outcome + / -
Friendship	Write book	05/10/2020	03/05/2021	+
Cooperation	Hobby	06/11/2020	N / A	
Integrity	Career			
Charity				

The table above is an example of a chart that you could make to record your top values, goals and possible outcomes with start and end dates if applicable. You can make the chart or journal entry as simple or complex as you like. The idea here is that when you have something on paper it becomes more concrete for you because you see it in the real world and it is not just some abstraction in your mind that you might get to "someday".

Our world is full of armchair doers – people that say "I am going to do that tomorrow", but tomorrow becomes the next day and the next day, and soon, the possibility extends into next month or next year. You do not want to be one of those people or you would not have picked up this book. Decide, commit and follow through. That is one of the secrets to success. It is not about money or fame or fortune. If you want to do something, first do it for you before even considering any other reason.

Knowing your purpose means you have a reason to get up every day! You know what you are going to do, and you are excited to do it!

KNOW YOUR "IKIGAI" (YOUR PURPOSE)

Make your purpose something specific

Make your goals measurable and quantifiable

You may say to yourself, "I have a job" or "I provide for my family" and that is great but when things get difficult, is it enough to get you out of bed and excited about every day?

The women of Okinawa Japan know what their IKIGAI is and they form social groups to encourage each other. This provides them with a sense of community and cooperation daily.

If you would like to learn more about why purpose is important look at the book, "The Power of Purpose" written by Richard J. Leider and Published by MJF Books.

There is absolutely nothing wrong with purely pleasure based happiness. Life is short. You need to discover what it is that makes you happy and try to fill your life with activities that bring you that sense of joy and fulfilment. Whether it is riding "Goliath" at Six Flags Great America Park, bicycling along your local community trail or singing in an 'a cappella' group. The key here is to discover what makes YOU happy and do more of it.

TO SUMMARIZE THE THREE STRANDS OF HAPPINESS [54]

1. Pleasure
2. Purpose
3. Pride

Your purpose references your drive or passion about something

Your pleasures are about your positive emotions about things

Your pride talks about your sense of satisfaction about your life as it is now

Being happy in your life potentially means that you will also live longer. Maximizing the time that we have on this planet not only means that we could potentially do more, but it means that you are using all the time that has been given to you to its maximum benefit for yourself and, by extension, what you do for others.

Many times, recommendations for health, happiness and longevity develop naturally from things like seeking a healthy lifestyle, proper diet, moderate alcohol and the reduction or elimination of smoking. These are all practical things. For example, most people agree that friends and family are important, but how many times do you sacrifice time with those you love because of work commitments or just not making that a priority for you? There is no magic here, just prioritizing what is most important and discarding the rest for another day or later that same day.

There are significant possibilities to make improvements in areas like finance, happiness at home, self-improvement, entertainment, work and social venues.

For example, key components to a happier community include:

1. Clean water
2. Choosing fruits and vegetables over fast food
3. Limiting billboards
4. Abundant sidewalks
5. Bike friendly lanes, paths and trails
6. High volunteerism
7. Many parks and green spaces

When the above-listed are checked off one by one, our communities will become friendlier, happier places that we will take pride in and enjoy showing to other people. This may even lead to increased tourism and holiday travel for the state, province or municipality.

Let us talk for a moment about a somewhat difficult but necessary subject finances and debt. Many people all over the world experience incredible amounts of stress and worry over their financial condition. Sometimes it is easy to believe that you are I are in control because we are making the minimum payments required by our creditors. That should never be good enough.

It is usually awfully hard to admit that you or I have a problem that needs to be recognized and conquered. Many people who have financial problems do not want to admit them either to themselves or other people, nor do they want to deal with them the way they should. Not only would dealing appropriately with financial challenges lead to less worry, but it also means that, instead of servicing a massive debt of between 18 and 22% on the average consumer credit cards, you can spend more of that money on things that matter more to you, your family and your friends.

Here are Seven simple steps to improve your financial position

1. Examine what you are paying out daily, weekly and monthly
2. Set a reasonable budget that leaves back 5 to 10% of what you earn for emergencies
3. Record your incoming monies and outgoing expenses
4. Pay down any balances owing on the highest interest credit card first
5. work to reduce or eliminate credit card debt
6. Use the '50-20-30' Rule – Set aside 50% of your income for essential expenses, 20% for debts and 30% for shopping and entertainment.
7. Seek professional help such as a credit counsellor or debt insolvency trustee if your debt becomes too large for you to manage

When your financial concerns are reduced in combination with other steps talked about in this chapter such as designing your space for a happier more productive lifestyle, looking for ways to live a healthier lifestyle, and making friends and family a priority, you will see your own positive sense of well-being increase exponentially. Other people will want what you have, and you can teach them using some of the skills you learn in this book.

Changing the world begins by changing one person at a time. When we change ourselves and become better, more positive and happier people, then the way we see the world changes with us.

Personal growth and maturity are often gradual, but when others see it in you and question how and why you are different, you will want to accelerate the positive changes and look for ways to improve all areas of your life:

Mental – What and how you think

Emotional – How you react to things around you

Physical – Improvements to your health, diet and exercise

Relational – How you relate to your spouse, children and others

Spiritual – Faith and Beliefs strengthened or challenged

You will see the world both as it is and how you would like it to be. Possibility and promise make the future more inviting. A positive, no limit person shapes the world by getting everyone in their sphere of influence excited. People around them cannot help but be changed and transformed. This transformative power exists within you and me. It is an unstoppable force!

You do not need to be Mother Teresa, Bill Gates, Malala Yousafzai, Nelson Mandala, or John Glenn to change the world. The power for change is inside each of us. The people that make the biggest difference look for opportunities and step up to the challenge. Make a difference for those in your family, your friends and your community today.

Remember the difference the people of Boulder, Colorado made for their state. They became a model for leaders around the country, other states and the world!

This chapter talks about special places around the world – the blue zones, where happiness is not an elusive, abstract concept, it is a lifestyle and the people who have embraced the blue zones philosophy are justifiably proud of their achievements.

ACTION STEPS

1. Name the 3 places that consistently rank among the happiest in the world?

2. What are three ways to scientifically measure happiness? These are also the "Three Strands of Happiness" that Dan Buettner defines in his book "The Blue Zones of Happiness"

3. What does the "Cantril Self-Anchoring Striving Scale" measure?

4. What is the formula Richard Leider teaches that will help you discover your purpose in life?

5. What is the "50-20-30" rule?

6. What are the "Power 9 Rules of Happiness"

7. Take the "Blue Zones of Happiness Test" for yourself at https://apps.bluezones.com/happiness to see your own level of happiness

8. Write down your top five values for the next one, two and five years

9. Write down two small things you can do today, tomorrow, next week and next month that will move you closer to your goals.

These must be small, definable and quantifiable steps (something that you can see accomplished and not something abstract)

10. Begin a small journal or diary about your own thoughts about happiness. This way you will see the positive changes that you are experiencing in your well-being and happiness levels

CHAPTER EIGHT

CONCLUSION

Happiness is "a state of well-being or contentment (and, most often), a pleasurable or satisfying experience"[55], and any dictionary can give you a definition, but how do you get to 'happy', especially in a world that is increasingly negative, pessimistic, harsh, opportunistic, selfish, often rude, egocentric, angry and deeply troubled?

There is so much negative thought that it is hard to find happiness represented well today. When someone is demonstrating outward signs of true happiness and joy, they might even be thought of as a rarity, an oddity or an exception! Truthfully, as we have seen throughout this book, they are not!

Happy people are everywhere, and their attitude of joy and simple pleasures is contagious! Throughout this book, you have seen examples of the people Wayne Dyer calls "no limit people". These people do not put limits on themselves or others and they see potential and possibility everywhere they look! The no limit person practices one of the first metrics of happiness – positive attitude. They know that, although our brains are wired biologically to be on guard for ever present dangers, our modern world, especially in the West in the last 50 years has eliminated many potential risks. No longer do you have to go hunting for food. It is artfully arranged on supermarket shelves.

Modern architecture and construction have eliminated other problems our ancestors faced due to weather and climate change because modern homes are built of firm foundations, cement and brick. These homes are insulated to keep you warm in the winter and cool in the summer. Our basic needs as identified by Maslow in his hierarchy of needs – food water and shelter being principal among them are met in many places around the world. Social programs mean that even the poorest among us in North America have a better standard of living than many in the poorest nations.

It is usually true that most middle and upper class North Americans have no excuse not to maintain a good attitude because so much of our lives are generously provided for through work, a social safety net for those who find themselves unemployed unable to work, and, access to technology and medicine to maintain good health over the long term.

Guard your attitude against things like:

- negative, self-defeating thoughts
- increasing violence around the world
- evidence of soil erosion and climate change
- pessimistic worldviews
- declining economic prosperity
- increasing health concerns such as those caused by the coronavirus of 2019

Everything on the list preceding our real concerns in our world today. You cannot deny that reality. You may feel things are out of control and spiraling downward, but you can control how you react to anything that happens to you. You have a choice. You can react negatively and be at the mercy of your emotions or, you can, as Rachel Hirschberg correctly observed in her book "Activating Happiness" , stop, think before you react so that you can get to know yourself and what tends to overwhelm you. She said as noted earlier in this book that when you control your

TRAPS

TRIGGER

RESPONSE

ACTION PATTERN

CONSEQUENCES

When you can recognize how you feel in given situations and take a moment to step back then your triggers and negative responses will not control you. When you know, for example that every time you are with Mrs. Smith that she talks about how much more polished and practiced her son is at the guitar than your daughter is on the drums in their band, and you feel your blood pressure rising, you simply smile, turn away for a moment and count to 10 in your mind before you turn back and say, "Yes, John is wonderful in the trumpet, but Beth is awesome on the drums too!"

Part of becoming a happier person is recognizing that you should try to focus on external things that you can control. When you do that you give the control part of your brain time to react positively to a situation which might have otherwise turned out negatively. Remember the six-step process that Rachel Hershenberg presents in "Activating Happiness":

The Six Step Process [56]

1. Notice the Choice Point
2. Do not Act, Breathe
3. What is the best way to nurture myself so that I will feel better about this situation?
4. Choose your behavior
5. ask immediately, "how did the situation serve me?"
6. Later asked, "how did the situation serve me overall?"

Remember the importance of discovering your true purpose, that thing the Okanogan people call, "IKIGAI" because when you discover your purpose you have reason to get up in the morning. Knowing what your purpose is helps to bring you joy.

Discovering your purpose also means that you can decide what is important to you! Having things in your life that matter helps align your goals and your values. Knowing what matters to you means that you can try to avoid those things that do not and remove the clutter and unnecessary things in life including negative people and those things that waste your time. How can you gain precious time in your life? Paradoxically you can gain time by limiting it as we discussed earlier in this book. Time will fill whatever vacuum it has for itself. Therefore, giving yourself a deadline and reducing the time available to complete something means that you will be more productive and happier.

It is not my intention to repeat what I have already said in this book. I DO want to remind you of some of these key aspects to developing your sense of well-being and ultimate joy and fulfilment that we have been talking about here

No feelings are ever permanent! Change is always possible! Everyone makes mistakes and the biggest successes are arrived at by those people that make the most mistakes. The biggest failure to happiness is probably not to try. Thomas Edison should be our example -- 10,000 failed attempts are 10,000 things that did not work! Keep moving forward. Look for possibilities and try every day to make a difference. You will not succeed at everything you attempt but everything you do puts you on a path to even greater future success and that happiness you deserve.

There is a recent movement called "We Day" This is an annual event dedicated to empowering youth to positive change in the world around them. Every year since "We Day" began in 2007 by brothers Mark and Craig Keilburger, life altering, and positive events have been undertaken by young people hungry for a positive change and dedicated to better. We Day is described as:

"an annual series of stadium-sized youth empowerment events organized by We Charity (formerly known as Free The Children), a Canadian charity founded by brothers Marc and Craig Kielburger. WE Day events host tens of thousands of students and celebrate the impact they have made on local and global issues."[57]

The Keilburger brothers saw an opportunity to make the world a better place and they followed up their ideas with action. The result is thousands of people were changed and their positive actions realized and impacted many.

Alongside its initiatives in schools, the WE organization has a charity component (The WE Charity) and the "Me too We" Project component that engages in projects around the world that empower people worldwide and change their lives. Organizations like WE are helping to create a sense of well-being and happiness because the positivity becomes contagious.

One of the critical statements emphasized by the WE organization is "Be the change that you want to see!" and this speaks to you and I (individually and collectively) being the agent or catalyst for change. This distinction is crucial because it places things back into our control.

Happiness is inside each of us waiting to flourish. Most people want to be in control of their own lives and happiness. This book is about showing you ways that you can develop your own sense of positive well-being and joy anytime and anywhere. You have seen that you can train your brain to be happy by remembering, for instance that there are always things to be grateful about. When we do for others, we feel better about ourselves and when we meditate (take time away) in quiet, intentioned thought, this helps to bring us a sense of peace and calm.

You have seen that material wealth does not bring happiness. Material wealth simply brings you more choices. Scott Galloway has one of the best definitions of "rich". He says, "rich is having passive income greater than you burn"[58] and by that definition, many people are more well-off than they realize. Having a source of income that is "passive" (self-generating) means doing something once and income continues to flow. Discipline yourself to spend less and do more with what you already have.

It is a healthy balance between desire and contentment. Never stop fighting your internal conflict between "wanting more" and "having enough". There is often a fine line between want and desire and greed and selfishness. Every one of us must evaluate our own intentions against reality. Attitudes, values and beliefs very, but absolutes do and should exist. Laws in our society are all about absolutes that we as a collective group are committed to maintaining. When you think about your own personal happiness as it relates to specific goals and values that you set for yourself, make every effort to make sure that no one else is hurt intentionally or unintentionally by the paths that you choose for yourself.

Treat others the way you would want to be treated yourself. Practice random acts of giving at every opportunity. Those receiving your kindness will usually appreciate the gesture and this will foster in them a desire for change themselves. Growth is important on any level. Growth happens because of changes in perceptions. What you once believed to be true, you realize now, is not. If you stop growing your path toward happiness is stalled. It is important to believe in the best possible outcome in any situation regardless of initial appearances. Change yourself and everything around you will change too!

Life is a journey. Embark on it with confidence and courage. Believe and expect the best, always! Demonstrate a willingness to compromise when your views conflict with those of other people. The only thing in life that you can control is yourself. There are no guarantees in life, but the "no limit person" consistently tries to turn everything into a "good" outcome. If you catch yourself becoming anxious, take a moment, reframe your thoughts into positive ones and act the way you would if your thoughts had already transformed.

Many people recognize early the importance of having a positive role model in their lives. They have committed to following the advice of a mentor. A mentor is someone that you respect and are willing to pattern your life alongside. Decades of life lessons can be incorporated into your own life much more easily than if you had to learn many of these things on your own. This not only shortens the learning curve but allows you to incorporate the best into your life in a much more protracted way. You are not copying them. You are becoming an amalgamation of the best that you see in them and conversely, those elements that are the best in you are becoming reflected in them too. The important role that a mentor plays in your life, means that it is particularly important to choose one wisely. Tell the person that you have chosen as your mentor of your intentions to emulate them, communicate their importance in your life and make sure they approve of the responsibility of acting in such a role for you. A person of such importance in your life should have equal respect for you and therefore be understanding and totally committed to your well-being and happiness!

Earlier in this book the importance of taking personal responsibility for everything that happens in your life was emphasized. It is only through taking complete responsibility that you stop blaming and criticizing others for all that is wrong in your life. When you do this, you free yourself to recognize that it is the choices you and I make, even if initially less than ideal can be modified to achieve more satisfactory outcomes in every aspect of our lives.

Everyone is given one lifetime to live as they wish. Know that life is finite. Because of the limits that time places on all of us, it is important to make wise and considered decisions about how we spend it. There are negatives to either end of the widest spectrum. Do not be too rigid nor too lax in your approaches. Do what you feel is appropriate for you and where you are at this moment, but always be willing to change if this will potentially result in a better outcome for you or those in your sphere of influence.

Our society tends to believe that we have all the answers. This is far from true. We are small in comparison to the reality that there are approximately 600,000 stars in our galaxy alone and, of the approximately 7 billion people currently on the earth and an estimated 15 billion people who have ever lived in the history of the world, [59]our place is small but we can collectively impact others both now and for generations if we try at every opportunity to do "good", care for others and look for the best in everyone.

No masterpiece is ever complete in one day. You have an entire lifetime (however long that is) to grow, mature, fail, try again, improve, endure difficult times, change your approach and succeed again before your life concludes in its present reality. You may reinvent yourself several times along the way when you correct what is not working for you and move forward. Do not stop. Keep going as long as you have breath and will. Others will be encouraged by your persistence and perseverance.

Be thankful for wherever you are in your life. Be thankful for the good things. Appreciate all the people that helped form who you are now and who we will become. In the entire population of the world there is no one exactly like you.

Celebrate you! Contribute in your own unique way to make this world a better place than it was before you came along. When you live each day trying to do good, make a difference and choose sometimes to put the good of someone else ahead of yourself, then happiness will be the result. When your personal priorities are in line with your goals, values and beliefs and you are actively looking for opportunities to help others, this win – win scenario is good for everyone.

One final insight is that –

"... achieving a state of wellness and activating happiness is a dynamic process. Wellness is a set of behaviours that shape and are shaped by your ever-changing environment."[60]

So, it is okay to be discouraged temporarily but do not stay there – at that point. Acknowledge your low point, see what has brought you there, and take the steps necessary to get out of that negative circumstance.

There are many things that we can choose to focus on in life. Whatever you focus on consistently will become your reality.

Ralph Waldo Emerson said, "for every minute you are angry, you lose sixty seconds of happiness."[61] Choose happiness! Focus on making happiness a priority in your life and it will become one. Sometimes it is as simple as that!

It is my hope that you found value in this book. If you did, please consider submitting a review to the bookseller where you found it. Taking a few minutes to submit a review gives others a chance to discover this book for themselves and perhaps create more happiness in their own life as a result.

Remember, this book is a work in progress. Future editions will incorporate changes and revisions that will make it a better, more accessible work. Thank you for taking the time to read and practice some of its suggestions and "action steps" along the way. Success builds success. The results achieved in anything are directly proportional to the effort applied. If you put in massive effort to practice the principles explained in this book, you will see results!

There are thousands of books that have been written about happiness. This means that I can only include things that I thought were most important for you to discover about the topic. For your convenience, I have included a list of further resources to enhance your study and understanding of happiness. Please take time to review this and decide where your journey continues from this point.

It is because of my own personal interest in the subject of happiness that compelled me to write this book. Your own journey will take you in many different directions and that is wonderful! Where you are five years from now will be in a different place than at this moment. Notice the differences and welcome changes as part of the learning process. Change is not always easy. Challenges build character when they are eventually defeated and overcome.

When you look back, and you say, "I got through that and I can get through this in my life too!" and that experience will embolden you to take on new challenges. Do not turn away from them even when they are hard. Others are watching how you react in everything you do. Be the example you wish others had been for you. Always be willing to admit when you are wrong but be equally willing to be pleased with what you do right.

Get out there and meet the world head on! Be a 'no limit' person! Smile much more often than you frown and live your life with passion, bravado and gusto!

ACTION STEPS

1. What is the definition of happiness that is presented at the beginning of this chapter and throughout the book?

2. What is 'a no limit' person? How is someone who does more than what would normally be expected of them related to this?

3. Identify some of the negative things in the world today that try to rob you of your sense of joy and happiness?

4. How can you use Dr. Rachel Hershenberg's method of identifying T.R.A.P.S. help you find and eliminate things that only make you feel powerless and afraid, but prevent you from positive change?

5. Why is maintaining a good attitude so important to your overall level of Happiness?

6. Define the term "IKIGAI" Write down what you believe your own personal IKIGAI is ...

7. What is "WE DAY"? What are some personal projects that you can begin, even on an exceedingly small level, to do some 'good' in your community or state?

8. What can you take from this summary chapter that you can use today?

9. Start a personal diary or blog to chart your happiness journey. Blogger (www.blogger.com) is a great place to start. (See the "Resources" section following this chapter for more ideas)

RESOURCES

1. The Happiness Lab https://www.happinesslab.fm/

This is a podcast from Dr. Laura Santos, a professor at Yale University that covers almost every area of the science of Happiness. Highly Recommend

2. "The Science of Well Being" is a University course on the science of happiness. It became so popular among students that it can now be audited for free by anyone online at https://www.coursera.org/learn/the-science-of-well-being

If you want documentation that you completed the course, paid options are available, but anyone can select the free option and take the course.

3. The Institute for Global Happiness. "https://globalhappiness.org/resources/

One of the authors referenced in this book, Neil Pasricha, created a Global Happiness Institute". The organization's mission is to improve happiness levels inside organizations.

4. Top 10 Happiness Resources

http://www.huwrichardscoaching.com/top-ten-happiness-resources-on-the-web/

Here is a list of 10 Important happiness resources including the VIA instate that is also referenced in the Science of Well-Being" Course above

5. Live Happy Now is a wonderful online happiness resource for articles, podcasts and information about happiness. You can find "live Happy Now" at www.livehappy.com

6. Happy Brain Science
   https://www.happybrainscience.com/resources/

Is a great resource for information about happiness. The mission of this group is to "to foster productivity, creativity and happiness through the application of cutting-edge brain science

7. Best Free Blog (Web LOG) like a personal writing space on the web.

https://themeisle.com/blog/best-free-blogging-sites/

Bibliography

A Conscious Rethink. "10 Things That Make A Person Unique,"
April 26, 2019. https://www.aconsciousrethink.com/10341/10-
things-that-make-a-person-unique/.

Adelina Tuca. "9 Best Free Blogging Sites in 2020 (Create a Blog
for Free)." *Themelsle Blog* (blog), May 21, 2020.
https://themeisle.com/blog/best-free-blogging-sites/.

Buettner, Dan. *The Blue Zones of Happiness: Lessons from the
World's Happiest People".* National Geographic Partners, 2017.

Christine Chan. "Best Journaling Apps for iPhone and iPad in
2020." Technology Reviews and Information. iMore, January 8,
2020. https://www.imore.com/best-journaling-apps-iphone-and-
ipad.

Fandom TV Community. "Girl Meets World Wiki." Girl Meet World
Wiki, 2020.
https://girlmeetsworld.fandom.com/wiki/Girl_Meets_World_Wiki
.

Finkelstein, J. *Diagram of Maslow's Hierarchy of Needs.* October
27, 2006. I created this work using Inkscape.
https://commons.wikimedia.org/wiki/File:Maslow%27s_hierarchy
_of_needs.svg.

Foundation, Poetry. "The Road Not Taken by Robert Frost."
Text/html. Poetry Foundation. Poetry Foundation, May 15, 2020.
Https://www.poetryfoundation.org/.
https://www.poetryfoundation.org/poems/44272/the-road-not-taken.

Goodreads. "Happiness Quotes (14171 Quotes)," 2020.
https://www.goodreads.com/quotes/tag/happiness.

———. "Thomas A. Edison Quotes (Author of St Agnes' Stand),"
2020.
https://www.goodreads.com/author/quotes/3091287.Thomas_A_Edison.

Hogenboom, Melissa. "The Traits That Make Human Beings
Unique," July 6, 2015.
https://www.bbc.com/future/article/20150706-the-small-list-of-things-that-make-humans-unique.

Huw Richards. "Top Ten Happiness Resources on The Web." *Huw
Richards Coaching* (blog), November 25, 2017.
http://www.huwrichardscoaching.com/top-ten-happiness-resources-on-the-web/.

StarWars.com. "Jabba the Hutt," 2020.
https://www.starwars.com/databank/jabba-the-hutt.

Girl Meets World Wiki. "List of Girl Meets World Episodes." Wiki.
Accessed May 14, 2020.

https://girlmeetsworld.fandom.com/wiki/List_of_Girl_Meets_World_episodes.

Mark Terry. "Compare: 1918 Spanish Influenza Pandemic Versus COVID-19." BioSpace, April 2, 2020. https://www.biospace.com/article/compare-1918-spanish-influenza-pandemic-versus-covid-19/.

Neil Pasricha. *The Happiness Equation: Want Nothing + Do Anything = Have Everything*. New York, New York: G.P. Putnam's Sons, 2016.

Science Fiction & Fantasy Stack Exchange. "Now That the Star Wars Franchise Belongs to Disney, Who Owns the Rights to Star Wars the Clone Wars?" 2020. https://scifi.stackexchange.com/questions/122022/now-that-the-star-wars-franchise-belongs-to-disney-who-owns-the-rights-to-star.

Pelerno, Elizabeth, and Rachel Ross. "Who Invented the Light Bulb?" livescience.com, August 17, 2017. https://www.livescience.com/43424-who-invented-the-light-bulb.html.

Rachel Hershenberg. *Activating Happiness: A Jumpstart Guide to Overcoming Low Motivation, Depression or Just Feeling Stuck*. Oakland, |California: New Harbinger Publication, Inc., 2017.

Regina. "What Makes Us Unique: Embrace Your Differences •
Regina Hypnotherapy." *Regina Hypnotherapy* (blog), August 29,
2019. https://reginahypnotherapy.co.uk/what-makes-us-unique/.

Renee Cherry. "These Journal Apps Will Turn You into a Total
Documentarian." Shape, September 24, 2019.
https://www.shape.com/lifestyle/mind-and-body/best-journal-
apps.

Scott Galloway. *The Algebra of Happiness*. New York: Penguin
Random House, 2019.

Wayne Dyer. *Happiness Is the Way*. Carlsbad, California: Hay
House Publishers, 2019.

"World Population Clock: 7.8 Billion People (2020) -
Worldometer," 2020. https://www.worldometers.info/world-
population/.

ENDNOTES

[1] https://www.merriam-webster.com/dictionary/happiness?src=search-dict-box

[2] "Happiness is the Way", Wayne Dyer, Hay House Publishers, Carlsbad, California, 2019. P. xiv

[3] https://www.merriam-webster.com/dictionary/choices

[4] "Happiness is the Way: Wayne Dyer, Hay House publishers, Carlsbad, California, p.3

[5] Happiness is the Way: Wayne Dyer, Hay House publishers, Carlsbad, California, p.23

[6] Happiness is the Way", Wayne Dyer, Hay House Publishers, Carlsbad, California, 2019, P.11.

[7] "Happiness is the Way", Wayne Dyer, Hay House Publishers, Carlsbad, California, 2019, P.13

[8] "Ten Things That Make a Peron Unique and Different", A Conscious Rethink, https://www.aconsciousrethink.com/10341/10-things-that-make-a-person-unique/

[9] Wikipedia, Wikipedia.org (illustration), creative commons license, https://commons.wikimedia.org/wiki/File:Maslow%27s_hierarchy_of_needs.svg

[10] The Happiness Equation: Want Nothing + Do Anything = Have Everything", Neil Pasricha, G.P. Putnam's Son's, New York, 2016, p.81

[11] "the Happiness Equation: Want Nothing + Do Everything = Have Everything, Neil Pasricha, G.P. Putnam's Son's, 2016, P.220.

[12] "Activating Happiness: A Jumpstart Guide to Overcoming Low Motivation, Depression or Just Feeling Stuck", Rachel Herzenberg, New Harbinger Publications, Inc., Oakland, California, 2017, P.25.

[13] "Activating Happiness: A Jumpstart Guide to Overcoming Low Motivation, Depression or Just Feeling Stuck", Rachel Hershenberg, New Harbinger Publications, Inc., Oakland, California, 2017, p.5.

[14] "Activating Happiness: A Jumpstart Guide to Overcoming Low Motivation, Depression or Just Being Stuck.", Rachel Hershenberg, New Harbinger Publications, Inc, Oakland, California, 2017, P. 28.

[15] "Activating Happiness: A Jumpstart Guide to Overcoming Low Motivation, Depression or Just Being Stuck.", Rachel Hershenberg, New Harbinger Publications, Inc, Oakland, California, 2017, P. 5.

[16] "Activating Happiness: A Jumpstart Guide to Overcoming Low Motivation, Depression or Just Being Stuck.", Rachel Hershenberg, New Harbinger Publications, Inc, Oakland, California, 2017, P. 75.

[17] "Activating Happiness: A Jumpstart Guide to Overcoming Low Motivation, Depression or Just Being Stuck.", Rachel Hershenberg, New Harbinger Publications, Inc, Oakland, California, 2017, P. 95.

[18] Meriam Webster Online Dictionary, https://www.merriam-webster.com/dictionary/decide

[19] Goodreads, "Thomas A. Edison Quotes",https://www.goodreads.com/author/quotes/3091287.Thomas_A_Edison

[20] "The Happiness Equation: Want Nothing + Do Everything = Have Everything", Neil Pasricha, G.P. Putnam's Sons, New York, 2016, P.23.

[21] Meriam Webster Dictionary, https://www.merriam-webster.com/dictionary/happiness?src=search-dict-box

[22] "The Happiness Equation: Want Nothing + Do Anything = Have Everything", Neil Pasricha, G.P. Putnam's Son's, New York, 2016, P.59

[23] "The Algebra of Happiness", Scott Galloway, Penguin Random House, New York, 2019, P.19

[24] The Algebra of Happiness", Scott Galloway, Penguin Random House, New York, 2019, P. 49.

[25] The Happiness Equation: Want Nothing + Do Anything = Have Everything", Neil Pasricha, G.P. Putnam's Son's, New York, 2016, P. 21.

[26] "The Happiness Equation: Want Nothing + Do Anything = Have Everything", Neil Pasricha, G.P. Putnam's Son's, New York, 2016, PP... 19-27.

[27] "The Happiness Equation: Want Nothing + Do Anything = Have Everything", Neil Pasricha, G.P. Putnam's Son's, New York, 2016, p.27

[28] "Compare: 1918 Spanish Influenza Pandemic Versus COVID-19", Mark Terry, BioSpace, https://www.biospace.com/article/compare-1918-spanish-influenza-pandemic-versus-covid-19/, April 2,2020.

[29] "Compare 1918 Spanish Influenza Pandemic Versus COVID-19", Mark Terry, BioSpace, https://www.biospace.com/article/compare-1918-spanish-influenza-pandemic-versus-covid-19/, April 2,2020.

[30] "The Happiness Equation: Want Nothing + Do Anything = Have Everything", Neil Pasricha, G.P. Putnam's Son's, New York, 2016, p.8.

[31] "Happiness is the Way". Wayne Dyer, Hay House Publishers, Carlsbad, California, 2019, P.6.

[32] "Happiness is the Way". Wayne Dyer, Hay House Publishers, Carlsbad, California, 2019, P.26.

[33] World-O-Meter", https://www.worldometers.info/world-population/, 2020.

[34] "Happiness is the Way", Wayne Dyer, Hay House Publishers, Carlsbad, California, 2019, P.3.

[35] Happiness is the Way", Wayne Dyer, Hay House Publishers, Carlsbad, California, 2019, P.77.

[36] Wikipedia, "Cerebral Palsy", https://en.wikipedia.org/wiki/Cerebral_palsy, 2020.

[37] Goodreads, "Thomas Carlyle Quotes", https://www.goodreads.com/quotes/174665-every-man-is-my-superior-in-that-i-may-learn,

[38] "The Road Not Taken", Robert Frost, The Poetry Foundation, https://www.poetryfoundation.org/poems/44272/the-road-not-taken

[39] Activating Happiness: A Jumpstart Guide to Overcoming Low Motivation, Depression or Just Feeling Stuck", Rachel Hershenberg, New harbinger Publications, Inc. Oakland, California, 2017, PP.160-161.

[40] "The Algebra of Happiness", Scott Galloway, Penguin Random House, New York, 2010, P.79.

[41] "The Algebra of Happiness", Scott Galloway, Penguin Random House, New York, 2010, P.60.

[42] The Happiness Equation: Want Nothing + Do Anything = Have Everything", Neil Pasricha, G.P. Putnam's Sons, New York, 2016, PP. 112-120.

[43] "The Happiness Equation: Want Nothing + Do Anything = Have Everything", Neil Pasricha, G.P. Putnam's Sons, New York, 2016, PP. 116-118.

[44] "The Happiness Equation: Want Nothing + Do Anything = Have Everything", Neil Pasricha, G.P. Putnam's Sons, New York, 2016, P.22

[45] Wikipedia, Boulder Colorado, https://en.wikipedia.org/wiki/Boulder,_Colorado, 2020.

[46] "The Blue Zones of Happiness: Lessons from the World's Happiest Places", Dan Buettner, National Geographic Partners, 1145 17th Street. NW, Washington D.C., 2017, P.117.

[47] "The Blue Zones of Happiness: Lessons from the World's Happiest Places", Dan Buettner, National Geographic Partners, 1145 17th Street. NW, Washington D.C., 2017, P.118.

[48] "The Blue Zones of Happiness: Lessons from the World's Happiest Places", Dan Buettner, National Geographic Partners, 1145 17th Street. NW, Washington D.C., 2017 Excerpt from back book jacket cover.

[49] Wikipedia, "California", https://en.wikipedia.org/wiki/California, 2020.

[50] "The Blue Zones of Happiness: Lessons from the World's Happiest Places", Dan Buettner, National Geographic Partners, 1145 17th Street. NW, Washington D.C., 2017, P.22.

[51] "The Blue Zones of Happiness: Lessons from the World's Happiest Places", Dan Buettner, National Geographic Partners, 1145 17th Street. NW, Washington D.C., 2017, P.20
.

[52] "The Blue Zones of Happiness: Lessons from the World's Happiest Places", Dan Buettner, National Geographic Partners, 1145 17th Street. NW, Washington D.C., 2017, P.21.

[53] "The Blue Zones of Happiness: Lessons from the World's Happiest Places", Dan Buettner, National Geographic Partners, 1145 17th Street. NW, Washington D.C., 2017, PP. 247-249.
.

[54] "The Blue Zones of Happiness: Lessons from the World's Happiest Places", Dan Buettner, National Geographic Partners, 1145 17th Street. NW, Washington D.C., 2017, P.20.

[55] Happiness", Merriam-Webster Dictionary, https://www.merriam-webster.com/dictionary/happiness?src=search-dict-box, 2020.

[56] Activating Happiness: A Jumpstart Guide to Overcoming Low Motivation or Just Feeling Stuck", New Harbinger Publications Inc., Oakland, California, 2017, P.92.

[57] " WE DAY", Wikipedia, https://en.wikipedia.org/wiki/We_Day, 2020

[58] Scott Galloway, "The Algebra of Happiness", Penguin Random House, New York, 2015, P.26.

[59] "The Happiness Equation: Want Nothing + Do Anything = Have Everything", Neil Pasricha, G.P. Putnam's Sons, New York, 2016, P.89.

[60] "Activating Happiness: A Jumpstart Guide to Overcoming Low Motivation, Depression or Just Feeling Stuck", Rachel Hershenberg, New Harbinger Publications Inc., Oakland, California, 2017, P.161.

[61] "Happiness Quotes", Goodreads, https://www.goodreads.com/quotes/tag/happiness

THANK YOU

Thank you for purchasing this book!

 It is my sincere hope that you enjoyed reading it as much as I enjoyed writing it!

There are many books on the market about this topic but I have tried to draw from a variety of sources to give you an overview of some important things that I have discovered, have found value in, and believe you will too.

I wanted this book to be easy to read and something that you could pick up and even reread occasionally, if you found yourself slipping in all patterns of behavior, wanted a shift in attitude or action, or saw yourself slipping into a depressive or unhealthy state.

If you found this book useful in any way, please consider submitting a review at your place of purchase so that others may benefit also by learning what you found useful and perhaps purchase the book themselves.

If you have questions or comments you are welcome to submit them by email to steve@stevenmilbrandt.com

Manufactured by Amazon.ca
Acheson, AB

15888047R00074